New York Institution for the Blind.

stead of their eyes. the blind pick up
'e gems of thought with their fingers.
S. Helen De Kroyft.

A PLACE IN THY MEMORY.

With the year
Seasons return, but not to me returns
Day, or the sweet approach of ev'n or morn,
Or sight of vernal bloom, or summer's rose,
Or flocks, or herds, or human face divine.
MILTON.

BY MRS. S. H. DEKROYFT.

NEW YORK:
JOHN F. TROW, PRINTER AND STEREOTYPER,
377 & 379 BROADWAY.
1858.

TO

MRS. DOCTOR NOTT,

OF UNION COLLEGE, SCHENECTADY,

WHO FIRST SUGGESTED ITS PUBLICATION

THIS VOLUME

IS VERY AFFECTIONATELY INSCRIBED

By the Authoress.

PREFACE.

THESE Letters are simply copies of my own thoughts and feelings, written with no expectation of their ever being read by others than the persons to whom they were addressed. But as the author of the "Memoirs of my Youth" laid bare his "palpitating heart" to the world for the sake of dollars, so I have been induced to gather from my friends these fragments, and bind them into a book.

Three summers ago, I had perfect sight. I was in one short month a bride, a widow, and blind; yet Providence has made it needful for me to do something to provide for myself food and raiment.

Upon the loss of my sight, I was, through the influence of Senator Backus, of Rochester, allowed to spend one year at the New-York Institution for the Blind, which time expired last May; and I had not where to go, or a friend whose kindness my three years of dependence had not wearied. There was no alternative, and with many fears of success, I embarked in the little enterprise of publishing this volume, by soliciting subscribers who would give their names, and pay me in advance.

Accordingly, with my prospectus in my hand, I first waited upon the Board of Managers of the Institution, who lent me their influence, and sanctioned my efforts by subscribing for several copies each. The next day, I waited upon the gentlemen of the City

Hall, and encouraged by their kindness, thence passed on through Broadway, Wall, South, and most of the principal streets of the city; and now that my task is ended, and my little book is about going to the publishers, I have not an unpleasant memory associated with the whole affair. In the hurry of business, in the intricacies of law, and amidst problems half solved, gentlemen have laid down their pens, read my prospectus, written their names, and paid their money; and often escorted me to the door, and saw me safely down the stairs, perchance, directing my gentle guide where to find others as kind as themselves.

Gratitude is the purest of the heart's memories, and I can only offer to my friends, subscribers, purchasers, and all, my warmest thanks. I cannot compliment my own work; I shall leave it with an indulgent public. In perusing its pages, however, the reader must remember that they were either written with the sense of feeling, by means of a grooved card, and pencil, or prompted to a friend, from an overburdened heart.

S. HELEN DeKROYFT.

New-York Institution for the Blind,
September 25, 1849.

A PLACE IN THY MEMORY.

Rochester, April, 1848.

My precious Mother,—My whole heart is drawn out to you. When William was with me, I loved him more than all the world beside, but he is in the grave now, and my purest affections, mother, evermore are yours. If this frail body could move with the fleetness of thought, I would come to you now, and pillow my weary head on your bosom, and your soft hands would dry these tears from my poor eyes. Oh that I could open them once more, mother, and see your smiling face, and feel my spirit grow warm and gentle in the light of your eyes, and your looks of love. Tell me, dear mother, have you changed at all? Do you look as when I saw you last?

Oh, had I known that ere we should meet again, the light would leave me, how would I have gazed on your form, until on my spirit were engraved your every look and feature! You often come to me now, when dreams possess my thoughts, and then I tell you how sad it is to be blind, and how melancholy the long days and nights are, and how I sometimes almost pray to go into the spirit world, and mount the wings of light for ever. But mother, I bless God for a cheerful faith, and a heart all resigned. Whatever his hand orders is for the best. You taught me early to *know*, and try to *do*, the will of God; but, mother, to *suffer* it is another thing. I could climb the Rocky Mountains to teach the Indians, cross the seas, and live for ever with the Hindoos, and the task would seem light, and my burdens easily borne; but when I look along the current, of perhaps fifty years, of darkness, dear mother, my heart fails, and like the doubting Hebrew, I begin to sink. Then an *unseen arm* lifts me, and whispers, "Be still, and know that I am God." Yes, dear mother, what we do not know now, we shall know hereafter. In a few days, new hills and valleys will intervene, and your anxious cares for your child will be kindled anew. But be comforted; the widow's God will take care of me, the friend of the ravens will not leave nor forsake me, and ere long, I shall come to you again. My heart coaxes me to come to you now, but duty points another way. Things are not always what they seem. When Moses looked around, for the last time, upon the white tents pitched at the foot of the mountain, and pressed the hands of the sires who had grown gray in his friendship, and embraced the little ones whose hearts had budded into life in the light of his heavenly face; when he bade adieu to all that was dear, and began his journey up the weary side of Pisgah, he little knew that the clouds which overhung him would so soon break away, and the glories of the promised land burst upon his enraptured vision. Mother, so good may yet come to me; there may be in reserve a morning whose dawn is not yet begun. Faith is the blossom of the soul; it makes the doctrine of a future life a bright reality, keeps heaven near, and brings departed ones in speaking distance; it chases away the shades of grief, and puts fear to flight.

Dear mother, your parting words are still fresh in my memory, and your prayers and tears are locked in my heart. Your love is a sort of spirit robe that covers all my thoughts, and I wear it every where. Kiss little sisters and brother often for me, and let them never forget their sister Helen; but they must not think of me only as something sad and melancholy, for I am growing more cheerful now; sometimes I laugh almost as merrily as ever. Tell brother, when I come again he will gather wild flowers with me as before, and I can hear him say his lessons, and Nin and Mary will read for me, and write all my letters, and I will teach them some new songs, and tell them many stories. They must go to the library every week, and write me what they read.

Water-Cure, Long Island.

My good Friend Mr. Dean:—Let me thank you many times for your dear note of yesterday. How kind of you to think of me in your leisure moments, when they come to you so seldom! I have no new thing to write to you, save that to-morrow Dr. and Mrs. Nott leave for their home in Schenectady, and also a lovely family, Mr. and Mrs. Hardy and daughter, of Virginia, all of whom will be very much missed in our circle. Mrs. H—— is somewhat larger than myself; her complexion is a dark brunette; she has jet black eyes, and her raven tresses nearly touch the ground. Some say she is a descendant of Pocahontas, or Metoka as her father called her. I do love a real Southern character, it makes one so cordial, generous, and impulsive. Mrs. Hardy and myself have climbed these hills together, crossed valleys, and traversed winding footpaths, and waded the brooks, and plunged and bathed together, till she seems almost a part of myself. I shall miss her gentle hand and kind words every where. But they have arranged that I pass the month of May next at their pleasant home in N——, which I fancy will be a little round of delight, *almost* a dissipation. The winter looks dark and cheerless now, for as yet I know not where to pass it; but you see there is a bright spot for me in the spring-time; so I will go on, laughingly and gladly, as though I had a fortune secured, and nothing more to do in this life but live and be happy.

One little thing I must tell you: Mrs. Hardy promises when she gets to New-York to send me back a nice writing-desk for a keepsake. Will not that be a precious gift? and how I shall love the dear thing for her sake! Oh, why is every body so kind to me? I cannot be sad long at a time if I try; some tuneful voice always comes to cheer, and some gentle hand to guide and bless me.

Dr. S—— is anxious for me to remain here until I am quite well. He says the water treatment is much more effectual in cold weather than in warm. Besides, the good Quaker steward and stewardess often say, "I think we must keep thee here this winter, thou wilt be so much company for us."

New-York Institution for the Blind.

MY PRECIOUS MOTHER,

THE sun set upon the sea, and the moon rose above the hills, and the stars came out smiling through the clouds, like bands of angels, with linked hands, flying through the heavens. The reading hour past, we sang an evening hymn, and prayers were said, and the bell rang for ten, and all laid them down to sleep. To Him who sits enthroned in the abodes of light and love, I heard Mary's lips whispering of mother, home, and heaven. Perchance she is dreaming now of faces imaged on her heart long ago, and the sunny hours of childhood with their visions of joy have come to possess her thoughts. It is midnight, that deep hushed hour, when the soul turns back upon itself, and all the thoughts and feelings are chased homeward by incidents of the past. Now the night dews are hanging lightly on all the flowers, and the green leaves in moony shadows are trembling on the walls, and the lengthened forms of the waving boughs are crawling on the floor, as the shades of melancholy creep o'er my soul. Away yonder on the bosom of the Hudson the lights of the sky are twinkling; so up in heaven, on the fountain that wells from the throne, the smiles of God are playing. The world of spirits is opened to ours, and ours to theirs; even now, loved ones departed are in smiling distance, and their blent voices fall on my ear, like the pulses of a lute, when the waking hand has passed away. They come in the night time, when silence holds her spell-like reign, and in unseen communion spirit doth with spirit blend. Night too is the time for prayer; then the ear of Heaven is nearer bent, and the full sad heart, by faith, breathes a freer air, and leaping upward, gets new and clearer glimpses of the Christian's better life. So Jesus, wearied with the toils of the day, oft at night climbed lonely Olivet, apart to pray and talk with his Father in heaven, and seraphs who had grown old in his love were with him there; and while he kneeled upon the damp earth, their spirit hands dried his tears away. Dear mother, I often fancy you must be near, and turn to hear you speak, and put out my hand, but to greet the empty air. Oh, think of me when the morning breaks, and when the noon is bright, and the day declines; and pray for me too, lest this life of darkness make me sad, and loneliness' self settle on me. Write to me often, mother, and say I have always a place in your love, and a memory in your prayers; say that little brother and sisters speak of me in their play, and count the days until I shall come back again. I am pleased with the Institution. If Charity herself had come down to build on earth a home for her children, and Innocence had gathered them, the dwelling were not more fair, or its inhabitants more lovely and pure. But, dear mother, I love our blue Ontario more; its green shore inurns the stirring memories of a heart that was my own; besides, the dearest spot is always where our friends abide. When the sun was going down I went into the garden, and felt around among the bushes, until I found some flowers, and gathered a beautiful bouquet for you, mother, and now, in fancy, I will steal softly into your room, and lay it on your pillow. May its sweet perfumes make you dream of a land where flowers never fade, and those we love never die; where sorrow may not come, and where with a napkin of love all tears shall be wiped from our eyes.

Institution for the Blind, January, 1847.

THIS hour I sit me down to write you in a little world of sweet sounds. The choir in the chapel are chanting at the organ their evening hymn—across the hall a little group with the piano and flute are turning the very atmosphere into melody; but Fanny, the poetess, is not there. Many weeks her harp and guitar have been unstrung, and we fear the hand of consumption is stealing her gentle spirit away. In a room below, some twenty little blind girls are joining their silvery voices in tones sweet and pure as angels' whispers. And ah! here comes one who has strayed from their number the twentieth time to-day, clambering her little arms about my neck for a kiss. Earth has no treasure so heavenly as the love of a sinless child. Man seldom welcomes you farther than the fair vestibule of his heart, but a child invites you within the temple, where alone the incense of unselfish love burns upon its own altar.

'Tis evening—the moonbeams gladden all the hills, the stars are out and I see them not—once my poor eyes loved to watch those wheeling orbs, till they seemed joyous spirits bathing in the holy light of the clear upper skies :—but *now* they are not lost to me; fancy, with a soul-lit look, often wanders in the halls of memory, where hang daguerreotypes of all that is bright and beautiful in nature, from the lowest flower that unfolds its petals to the sunbeams, up to the cloud-capt mountain and the regions of the starry sky—whence she plumes her pinions, boldly entering upon new and untried regions of thought; passes the boundary of the unseen, to far-off fields where "Deity geometrizes," and nebular worlds are ever springing into new life and glory; and upwards still to the spirit land, where all are blessed and lost in present joys, till happiness, forgetful, numbers not the hours. There my thoughts love to linger, till with the angels I seem to come and go, wandering by joy's welling fountains and glad rivers of delight!

But oh! this is truth and not fancy. My life is a "night of years," and my path is a sepulchred way; on one side sleeps MY FRIEND, and on the other lies buried for ever a world of light, and all its rays revealed: the smiles of friends and all their looks of love, without which the heart knows no morning. The Saviour wept at the grave of his friend, and I know he does not chide these tears; they are the impearled dews of feeling which gather round a sorrowed heart. But where God sends one angel to afflict, he always sends many more to comfort; so I have many angel friends who love me well. Their gentle hands lead me by pleasant ways, and their tuneful voices read to me, and the kindness of their words makes my heart better. Oh! tell me; when summer gladdens the world and vacation gladdens me, shall I again be on the banks of the Genesee, the while loved and blessed by the warm hearts of Rochester?

Lake Cottage, November, 1847.

MY DEAR LIZZY:—It is not pleasant to be blind. My *poor eyes* long to look abroad upon this beautiful world, and my prisoned spirit struggles to break its darkness. I would love dearly to bonnet and shawl myself and go forth to breathe the air alone, and free as the breeze that fans my brow. But as Milton once said to his favorite daughter, "It matters little whether one has a star to guide or an angel-hand to lead;" and, Lizzy, we must learn to bear, and blame not that which we cannot change. The journey of life is short. We may not stop here long, and sorrow and trial discipline the spirit, and educate the soul for a future life; and those upon whom we most depend, we love most. A good English writer says, "Let thy heart be thankful for any circumstance that proves thy friend."

Two summers have come and gone since my William died in Rochester. We brought him here and laid him down in the grave to sleep, close by his childhood-home, where the quick winds and white waves of Ontario come swelling to the shore; and high above its silvery bosom, clouds, dove-like, are hanging. One moon had hardly waned, when the angels came again, and while I slept darkened my weeping eyes for ever. Oh! Lizzy, was sorrow ever so deep? was misery ever so severe? Hope departed, and an unyielding blight settled on all the joys my heart had wed. "Passing away" is truly a part of earth. It lends a deathlike air to our gay enjoyments, and mingles sorrow with our cups of bliss. It stops for ever our happy labors, and frustrates our choicest plans. Those whom we learn to love, die, and the cold earth presses the lips we have loved to kiss, and freezes the hearts tuned to beat in unison with our own. Lizzy, evermore I am blind, and a wanderer, but not homeless. I have God for my father, the angels for friends, and Jesus an "elder brother." The pure homes in many hearts, too, are mine—dwellings dearer than all the world beside.

This morning finds me at Mr. Ledyard's delightful "Lake Cottage," where Lombard poplars lift their tapering tops almost to prop the skies; the willow, locust, and horse-chestnut, spread their branches, and flowers never cease to blossom. Maggie is my kind amanuensis. Now she reads to me—gives me her arm for a walk. Now, with her harp and tuneful voice, she unchains the soul of song, the while covering all my thoughts with gladness, till I almost forget my "night of years," and live in a land where ever swells with melody the air, and sorrow and tears are unknown, save such as pitying angels weep. With Maggie all joys are less than the *one joy* of doing kindness. Her smile makes the sunshine of many hearts; the cloudless dawning of their new enjoyments.

It is Thanksgiving Day, Lizzy, and my thoughts have been wandering backward, far over the current of years. Reflection is indeed an angel, when she points out the errors of the past and gives us courage to avoid them in the future. Maggie is reading me the book of Job, and this evening my spirit more than ever looks up in thankfulness to God for the Bible, Heaven's purest gift to mortals. It is the star of eternity, whose mild rays come twinkling to this nether sphere; erring man's guide to wisdom, virtue, and heaven. The Bible is the book of books. In comparison Byron loses his fire, Milton his soarings, Gray his beauties, and Homer his grandeur and figures. No eye like rapt Isaiah's ever pierced the veil of the future; no tongue ever reasoned like sainted Job's; no poet ever sung like Israel's shepherd king, and God never made a man more wise than Solomon. The words of the Bible are pictures of immortality; dews from the tree of Knowledge; pearls from the river of Life, and gems of celestial thought. As the moaning shell whispers of the sea, so the Bible breathes of love in heaven, the home of angels, and joys too pure to die. Would I had read it more when my *poor eyes* could see. Would more of its pure precepts were bound about my heart, and I had wisdom to make them the mottoes of my life. The world may entertain its idea of a magnificent Deity, whose government is general, but let me believe in the Lord God of Elijah, whose providence is entire, ordering the minutest event in human life, and with a father's care arranging it for the greatest possible good. Yes, Lizzy, when storms gather, and my way is dark and drear, with no star to guide, nor voice to cheer, my sinking spirit finds refuge in the world-wide sympathies of a Saviour who did not chide Mary for her tears, and came himself to weep at the grave of his friend.

My dear Lizzy, I fear I have written you too long and too sad a letter; but, dearest, do not think me melancholy; like all the rest of the world I have more smiles than tears, more good than ill. Let me thank you many times for your kind invitations to be with you on New Year's Day at your new home, and for your gentle hint that *Santa Claus* will be there too. Maggie says his majesty will be in the country at that time, and I must stop here; however, I shall be with you, Lizzy; till then good-bye, with my unabated love.

P. S. Water is to nature what melancholy is

to the soul; beautiful in its mildness, but terrific and fearful in its wrath. When I began my letter, Ontario was sleeping in her beauty; but since then she has foamed and roared like a thing of very madness, and her long circling waves have overturned the seaman's home, and borne it far down where the dolphins sleep, and the bones of wrecked mariners lie thick on the ground.

To-day I took a long adieu of William's grave; Maggie led me there and left me alone awhile, to commune with the dead; and as the waves washed the bright pebbles to the shore and bore them back again, so the tide of memory swept over my heart its cherished hopes; and I watched them fall back into the sea of life, to return no more.

June 14, 1849.

MY DEAR MRS. FISHER,—Your letter was a darling little visitor. My heart has had many a sweet chat with its friendly words.

How glad it made me I cannot tell you. It is pleasant to be remembered. I regret that Mr. F——— could not find time to call, but such remissness of *duty* is always pardonable in a business man. Well, dear Jenny, "they tell me Spring is waking," and all nature is teeming with very gladness ; the leaves and buds and twigs with new life are swelling, the little brooks have unclasped their icy bands, and the lake waters have broken their magic fetters, and the waves again dance to the tunes the breezes play, and the little seeds in the warm earth, like loving hearts, are beating and struggling upward to the world of light and showers ; so may our hearts pant for the waters whose streams flow fast by the throne of God, and the smile of Him whose look makes the light of heaven.

You are going to your pleasant home ; may it be ever the resting place of peace and plenty, and may no ills come there, and no storms gather to mar your happiness. The days I passed with you are with me yet, like a dream of love which may not be told. True, joy did not crowd the hours with gladness, but all that souls can share we straightway embarked in a little commerce of heart, and felt ourselves growing richer by a perfect interchange of views and feelings. Locke, in all his reasonings, lived not half so fast. The world I live in is an ideal world, and its inhabitants are beings of fancy, and of course sinless and good; their lips speak no lies, and their hands work no evil; their smiles are like the beams of the morning, and their whispers like the night breeze among the flowers, soft and healing as the breath of prayer. Still, Jenny, this morning my imprisoned spirit would go into raptures for one glance at this world of light; oh yes, I would bow in grateful adoration for the fragment beam that plays idly on an infant's tear, or sports with a drop of dew. Oh holy light! thou art old as the look of God, and eternal as his breath. The angels were rocked in thy lap, and their infant smiles were brightened by thee. Creation is in thy memory; by thy torch the throne of Jehovah was set, and thy hand burnished the myriad stars that glitter in his crown. Worlds, new, from His omnipotent hand, were sprinkled with beams from thy baptismal font. At thy golden urn pale Luna comes to fill her silver horn, and Saturn bathes his sky-girt rings; Jupiter lights his waning moons, and Venus dips her queenly robes anew. Thy fountains are shoreless as the ocean of heavenly love, thy centre is every where, and thy boundary no power has marked. Thy beams gild the illimitable fields of space, and gladden the farthest verge of the universe. The glories of the seventh heaven are open to thy gaze, and thy glare is felt in the woes of lowest Erebus. The sealed books of heaven by thee are read, and thine eye, like the Infinite, can pierce the dark veil of the future, and glance backward through the mystic cycles of the past. Thy touch gives the lily its whiteness, the rose its tint, and thy kindling ray makes the diamond's light; thy beams are mighty as the power that binds the spheres; thou canst change the sleety winds to soothing zephyrs, and thou canst melt the icy mountains of the poles to gentle rains and dewy vapors. The granite rocks of the hills are upturned by thee, volcanoes burst, islands sink and rise, rivers roll, and oceans swell at thy look of command. And oh, thou monarch of the skies, bend now thy bow of millioned arrows and pierce, if thou canst, this darkness that thrice twelve moons has bound me. Burst now thine emerald gates, O morn, and let thy dawning come. My eyes roll in vain to find thee, and my soul is weary of this interminable gloom. My heart is but the tomb of blighted hopes, and all the misery of feelings unemployed has settled on me. I am misfortune's child, and sorrow long since marked me for her own. The past comes back, robed in a pall, which makes all things dark. The future seems a rayless night, and the world does not always deal gently, even with one so sorrowed.

The sea of feeling, however calm, may be rippled by a breath, swollen by a word, clouded by a look, and lashed into fury by an act. But love like thine, is slow to censure, suspects never, and believes not till evidence look her so full in the face that there be no room for mistake; and even then she teaches rather pity than blame, rather forgives than condemns, and lets compassion cover the errors

and faults that Charity cannot hide. Out of heaven, and the Bible, there is nothing so pure as that love which makes us forget ourselves and live unto others. The last time Eve wandered through Eden's bowers of celestial amaranth, the angels, betokening her departure, gave her many flowers, which she twined in her hair, and wore on her neck, all, save one, a love blossom, which she pressed to her breast, and the approving smile of all the angels quickened its fainting leaves into life, and it took root in her heart; and so, evermore, the children of Eve are inclined to love. * *
* * * * * * * * *

Rochester, July 1*st*, 1847.

MUCH-LOVED MRS. BUCKLEY, far away :—My Institution friends thought it presumptuous for me to journey to Rochester alone, and the Superintendent laughed when I told him the angels would take care of me. Their care was needful, too, for I began my journey quite unincumbered with money, ordinarily so essentia to the traveller. The GOOD, men do should be known; their better deeds often are told. The world has bad notions of itself; it is not a selfish, but an unselfish world—a kind, a loving, and a forgiving world—more sunshine than storms, more smiles than frowns or tears. Men oftener love than hate, oftener do good than ill. This is not the best world we are to know; but it is next the best, and only a step lies between. Heaven is near the good, so near that loved ones, who inhabit there, are with us still. Stars unseen hang over us by day; so spirits from beyond the sky hang round our pathway, whispering words kind as heaven, on every breeze that fans our ears. We hear and follow them, but, like Samuel, fancying some Eli is calling.

Wishing to call at Catskill, I went on board the *Utica*. Your father met me there, with blessings in his heart and hand. "May God preserve and protect you, and in due time return you to us," said he, and departed. The sun went down; the moon and stars, those symbols of love in heaven, were in the sky;

the air was calm and inviting, even to "spirits of purity." Those whose eyes are folded have a quicker sense than sight, by which they know and feel when a fixed gaze is on them. Only one lady remained with me in the cabin; at length, with her babe in her arms, she came, and placing her lips close to my ear, as if she thought me deaf, screamed, "Be you blind?" "Certainly," I said, smiling. Watching me a moment longer, she said, in a tone of satisfaction, "Well, I don't judge from your looks you feel very bad about it!" "No," I replied, "grieving never restores its object, so we must learn to bear, and blame not that which we cannot change." Presently a Miss, with a voice like music's self, placed her little hand in mine, saying, "It is delightful out; I know you cannot see the things we are passing, but I will describe them to you." I took her arm, and we were hardly seated on deck when the Captain joined our number, talking familiarly of the beautiful scenery which every where adorns the Hudson; "the proudest stream that journeys to the sea." "Yonder," said he, "is Washington Irving's delightful residence, so buried in shrubs and trees, one can only see the steeple; which has on it a weather-cock taken from the ship in which Major Andre was to have sailed." A gentleman is most eloquent when he has attentive lady listeners; and while we rode over the rippling waters, my thoughts gathered many new and beautiful images; and Memory, the mind's mirror, still treasures daguerreotypes of them all.

My visit in Catskill, with Mrs. Wilson and daughters, at their cottage home, was like a scene in a fairy land. As "distance lends enchantment to the view," so time enhances departed joys. On board the *Alida* for Albany, blind and alone, among strangers, I began to fear lest Mr. Dawson should not get my note and come for me at the boat. But the angels never fail to do their bidding. Strangers often prove the best of friends. "Lo! I am with you alway!" is not a promise, but a declaration. Mrs. Thomas, her husband and daughter, from New-York, recognizing my baggage-mark, sought me out; and, in their society, the hours went unnumbered by. When we stopped they would have taken me with them to Congress Hall, but the Captain kindly offered, if my friends should not come, to see me safe at his home. All left the saloon, but I had not waited long, when a gentleman with a kindly tread came, saying, "Your friend, Mr. D., is in Michigan, but, if you please, I will see you to his residence." He then secured my baggage, gave me his arm, and we were away, talking so familiarly of life, its changes, books, and places, that I forgot he was a stranger, and thought I had known him always. I knew by his voice he had seen many years, and by his words, as Pinckney says, he had

"A heart that can feel and a hand that can act."

He left, saying, "In the morning I will either come or send my son with a carriage to take you to the depot." My ministering angel, this time, was Thurlow Weed, of Albany; and, may the Lord add to the length of his days many happy years, and the joys of each succeeding be multiplied by the joys of the last!

In the forenoon, my seat in the car was shared by an aged sire, who beguiled the hours with pleasing incidents. In the afternoon, a Scotchman, from the banks of the Clyde, entertained me with descriptions of the Highlands. Eloquent lips are a good substitute for eyes. He was present when Leopold, in sable robes for his Charlotte, was ambassador for George the Fourth to Edinburgh. With the fleetness of fancy, I became not only a looker on, but an actor in all that brilliant scene. The splendid streets, and edifices, the dazzling crowd, the royal equipage, the high-headed and high-souled officers, the elegantly set tables and brilliant guests, he described as if with them but yesterday. Whoever he was, his happiness was greatest when contributing most to the happiness of others. It would have done your heart good to hear him repeat snatches from Burns, in the full spirit of the great Poet; who was, he said, one of Nature's own nobility. * * *

At Pittsford, resting by the way with friends of *lighter* days, a note from Mrs. H., of Rochester, welcomed me for a time to her home, where we read, ride, walk, and talk the days away. Lizzy and Mary, too, with gentle hands, come often to lead me by pleasant ways; now where the Genesee leaps thundering from the rocks, and now where it winds noiseless to the sleeping lake, always mentioning in words like pictures, every tree, shrub and flower. They tell me when we are at the corner of a new building, walking to the other gives its length, and knowing the number of stories, imagination readily makes the view her own; thus I keep in mind the many changes of our growing city. If Oswald's *Corinne* was more eloquent she was not more kind, nor her love more true. My poor eyes cannot see them, but I know looks of love are on their faces, such as pitying angels wear. Gratitude is the most heavenly inhabitant of the human breast, and though shut out from its beauties, it is still a blessing to exist in so good a world.

When the Autumn winds begin to moan among the trees, the members of the New-York Institution for the Blind will meet again at their happy home, where may the angels bring you often. Oh! you never seemed so near, so dear, as now. Accept my heart's love, sealed with a friendship's kiss. As Burns says, —"A heart-warm, fond good-by."

N. B. A lady never writes a letter without a postscript. I forgot to tell you that my journey home cost me nothing. Captains, railroad conductors and all, instead of presenting their bills, inquired how they could best serve me, where I would stop, &c. Ought not even the blind to be joyous and happy in a land so kind, so free, as ours?

* * * * *

Our nature is threefold, or in other words, we seem to be made up of three distinct beings, or sets of energies; mental, moral, and physical; and it is the strange mingling and commingling of these, and their effects and influences upon each other, that produce what is called character. When God made man, he did not intend his strongest powers should rule, but the best; but contrary to his wish, in most persons, the seat of government is planted in the mind instead of the heart; and reason is allowed to sway her glittering sceptre over those inhabitants of the soul, love, charity, gratitude, faith, and hope, which were intended to be free, or governed only by heaven's golden rules. Byron was an example in whose character it was difficult to say whether the mental or physical powers had the sway ; and so of Pope, and the selfish Walpole. Who, in reading the beautiful songs of Montgomery and Kirke White, does not feel that they came from a source entirely different. Indeed, in the one case we seem communing with spirits, whose very breath was warm with love from heaven; and in the other, with beings whose thoughts were inspired only in the gloom of night, and the sullenness of despair. Now education and manner of living have much to do with this. If books are placed before us which only encourage the ambition, and adorn and dignify the mind, and our food be such as stimulates and cultivates the less ennobling passions, though apparently simple in themselves, they are, nevertheless, in their effects lasting as eternity. A child, who before his morning meal has learned to whisper the name of Jesus in thank fulness and prayer, and at night holds his little heart up to God for blessings, when he grows to be a man will hardly go astray, or allow the impulses of his nature to be governed by a thing so cold and calculating as human reason; far otherwise; you will find him inquir ing of God, and his own conscience, the way of duty, and you will see him always forget ting himself and trying to make others happy. These thoughts are not too sober even for a school-girl; you are now building a character for yourself, of which the lessons and exercises of each day form a part. No after time can efface the consequences of one act, or the influence of one word, either upon ourselves or those around us. To get your lessons perfectly and recite them, is not all you have to do. A boarding-school is a little community by itself, in which each room answers to a dwelling, whose inhabitants we may call our neighbors; and here we have a field, into which we may bring into exercise all our capacities, both mental and moral. Here we may plant the germs of philanthropy and religious zeal; here we may learn to dry away the tear of sorrow, and smooth the pillow of the sick, and pity those who suffer. That beautiful command, that the strong should bear the infirmities of the weak, seems written almost expressly for the members of a school, for we cannot all gather knowledge with the same facility. A lesson that is sport for one, is a hard task for another. My dear, we have guardian angels who every day bear reports to heaven of our doings here, and when the books are opened we must answer for the record they have kept. From this hour, then, seek to know and do the will of your Heavenly Father. First see that your thoughts are clothed with the precepts of his word, and while you journey upward in life's mountain path, set on either side with briers and thorns, though your pilgrim feet may be often torn by flinty rocks you need not fear; for our Saviour has said, "Lo, I am with you always, even to the end of the world."

Rochester, Lizzy's Home.

THE friendship of the good is a refuge that fails not, a treasure that angels prize, and in their diadems it is set round with virtue, love, and truth.

My dear Augusta, as the flowers at eve incline their heads to departing sunbeams, so my spirit is drawn towards you, wander where I will. The love that does not end *in* this life, often ends with it; but the chain which binds our hearts has no broken links, and while life lasts, and beyond the sky, it will draw us together still. Loved one, where are you? Oh speak, I long to hear your words; they were music that fell on my ears and sank down into my heart, filling it with joys too much like heaven to fade or pass away. It is a long time since I have felt your friendly arms around my neck, and your kisses on my lips, and I often wonder if time and distance have not altogether estranged me from your thoughts. I know your *other self*, and those little ones who clamber by your side have right to the highest seat in your affections;

and your heart's temple, lighted by a mother's smile, should be to them earth's fairest home ; and there, dearest, I would have them ever stay and worship undisturbed at love's holiest altar, only let me share largely in your general love, and I shall be therewith content. But think of me sometimes, oftenest when you bow your heart at mercy's throne ;

> Ask for me heaven's blessings there,
> In the ardent hope of faith in prayer.

I am passing the winter far away by the Genesee, where with the wild flowers my infancy grew ; to-day the liquid thunders of its falls mingle with the winds ; and storms are gathering as on the day when you came first with books and papers to read to me in the New-York Institution for the Blind. No time or place is so dear to memory as where the sorrowed heart has been blest, and its burdens a while borne by another ; where the bereaved feelings have been coaxed to leave their sadness, and their tears dried by the hand of sympathy and love. A stranger in New-York, shut up in that school for the afflicted, how found I such a lodgment in your sympathies; and what spirit moved you to come so often to beguile my lonely hours; to take me to your pleasant home; to church, and every where I wished to go? If one good act pleases God more than another, it must be such forgetfulness of self, such desire to make others happy.

Last week Mr. and Mrs. H—— left Rochester for Boston. The day previous to their departure, the Sewing Society of their church met at the house of my venerable friend Dr. Brown. The weight of years is on him now, and his locks are changed to the gray filaments of wisdom; but his heart is young, and his mind is active as ever: and with the sweet consciousness of a life well spent, he waits only for his Master to call him home. Towards evening all the ladies were assembling in the Doctor's room, when Mrs. H——, ignorant of the cause, said to him. "Doctor, *you* seem to be the greatest attraction of the day;" whereupon an elderly lady entered, and approached Mrs. H——, bearing in her hand a silver waiter, and some napkin rings for her children. This needed no explanation; their choked feelings refused words; the light of the past was on them, and with these beautiful expressions of gratitude and love between them, they and all present wept over remembered kindnesses, and ties soon to be severed for ever. I said in my heart, behold how these sisters love one another, and no wonder; their joint labors have clothed the destitute, fed the hungry, blessed the sick, and relieved suffering of every order. In a word, they have long "shared each other's gladness, and wept each other's tears." In the evening Dr. Brown presented his son for baptism, a lad of some nine or ten years—the child of his old age. Several other parents did the same, and thus closed the labors of Mr. H. in Rochester. But the *good* that men do lives after them. Like bread upon the waters, if not realized now it will be gathered hereafter. When Mr. H. came to Rochester, his people were few in number, now they are a flourishing society; they have a beautiful church, an organ, and the largest parish library in the city.—But this is little, compared with the hundreds his indefatigable labors have saved from vice, and the many who by his precept and example have learned the luxury of doing good. I am passing a few days with my friend Lizzy at her new home.

My poor eyes did not see her exchange her hand for another's, but I heard her breathe her heart away in words low and truthful as angel vows. Her empire now is the domestic circle; her might is gentleness, and by it she winneth sway over all hearts that come within her borders. Lizzy is reading me Goldsmith, and as we turn his pages our gatherings are "*gold* all the way." It is safe reading authors one may love as well as their writings. Byron kindled his imagination by the dark and turbid waters of Acheron. Goldsmith wandered by the river of life, where from the fountain of his own feelings, and the society of the good, he gathered his pure thoughts, and his chaste and beautiful play of ideality, which instruct and enrapture the reader. Poor Goldsmith, poverty and want ever hung heavy at his heart; and his haunts still echo with his groans. But he went up the great highway to distinction, and wreathed upon his brow crowns woven of immortal laurels. Poverty is truly the cradle of genius; man obtains no excellence without labor. The master-spirits of all ages, who have dazzled the world with their brilliant achievements, had barriers to surmount, difficulties to remove, and only as they regulated their exertions by mental firmness did they become learned, great, or good. An ancient poet had for his motto, "The daring fortune favors." An American divine says, "In great and good pursuits, it is honorable, it is right, to use that kind of *omnipotence* which says *I will*, and the work is done."

Oh my dear Augusta, is it possible I am never to read any more? I forgot to bring a volume in raised print from the Institution, but passing one's fingers over the pages of a book is very unlike the glance of the eye. Last summer quite in the verge of autumn, my friend Mrs. Snow came with her ponies to take me riding. We crossed twice the Genesee, then pursued its windings, till we came where the sun's rays were turned away by the forest trees; and the sharp quick noise of the carriage wheels, changed to a muffled rumbling; and as we rode slowly over the winding roads, all was so sacredly silent there, the hushed breeze that stirred the leaves seemed the breath of prayer. It was Mount Hope, our beautiful home for the dead; and as we wandered among the tombs and monuments, my fingers read their inscriptions in grooved and raised letters.

"The most beloved of earth not long survive to-day."

My dear Franky lies there, and her darling babe is sleeping by her side; so quick sorrow treads upon the heels of joy. Grave-yards are solemn volumes, in which even the blind may read upon their marble pages the records of hopes all departed. Dear Augusta, mine hour of loneliness is passing now, and I feel reluctant to close this letter as I would an interview with yourself. When the flowers unfold their leaves, and the birds come back again, I shall return to the Institution, and resume my music. There I shall be far, far away from my Rochester friends, who are so kind, so very kind. I often think the world must have grown better since I could see. But, friend of my heart, you will come often to see me, and I shall love you well.

~~~~~

Institution for the Bind.

MY DEAR PARENTS FAR AWAY:—When I left your cottage home, the sleety winds of early Spring were blowing high, and the Crocuses were hardly yet above the ground. At your little threshold, you kissed me good-by, and I felt your tears warm on my cheeks. You pressed my hands, and father said, God bless you, my child, and I rode away. Words are not feelings, so I can never make you know the strange sensations that nestled in my soul, while I crossed the hills that windy day. Sometimes I fell into mysterious reveries, and fancied my journey home, my stay with you, and my departure, all an unfinished dream, and thought soon to awaken and find it so. Then I changed my position, and tried to open my eyes to see if the morning had not come.
~~~~~

Then I heard distinctly the rumbling of the stage wheels, the rattling of the harness, and the tread of the horses, and cracking of the driver's whip, and the frequent passing of farmers' teams; no I said this is *real*, I am not dreaming. Then I turned my face to the stage window, and felt the biting wind as it whistled by, but all around and above I could see nothing but clouds of folding darkness. Then I sank back, and my spirit reeled beneath the awful weight of conscious blindness which like a mountain seemed falling on me, and hiding me from the world for ever. Still I did not weep. I have no longer any tears to shed. My heart has known a grief so burning, that dews and moisture never more gather there. Like a seared forest its blossoms are all faded, and its leaves are withered and fallen * * * * *. I remain two weeks by the banks of the Guenaugua.

The night before my departure, some favored ones of Apollo sang under my window that sweetest of songs,

"We will welcome thee back again;"

and another, only one couplet of which I remember,

> "'Tis needful *we* watch thee by day,
> But the Angels will keep thee by night."

Professions of love and friendship cost us nothing. Words are wind, and feelings are only natural swellings of the heart; but acts are living things, like facts they are stubborn and everlasting, and good deeds are footsteps in the ladder which reaches heaven. I cannot count the days of my stay at Geneva, for happiness keeps no dial, and always forgets to number the hours. If the scenery of a place ever gives tone to the minds and hearts of its inhabitants, I am sure the beautiful Seneca has lent its look of love to those who dwell by its shore. On their homes may the rains and dews never cease to fall, and the light of health and peace never leave their brows. Eliza read to me nearly two volumes of Littell's Living Age. In one of the back numbers, Father, you will find a review of Swedenborg. I wish you would read it, and write me what you think of it. I send with this a volume of

Macaulay's Miscellanies. I know you will be pleased with what he says of the life and times of Milton and Cromwell. But in order to enjoy his reviews generally, one must divest his mind of all prejudice, and harbor only a spirit of liberal Christianity and free toleration; for such is certainly the spirit of the great author. The type is very fine, but I think, by the aid of your new glasses, you will be able to read it. But you must remember, Father, that your physical energies are not what they were twenty, or even ten years ago; besides, eyes both younger and stronger than yours are often materially injured by lamp light. Mary must read for you evenings; that will relieve you and improve her. Nin writes that she has nearly completed the works of Hannah More, and the poems of Mrs. Hemans. Though she may never possess the elegance and varied learning of the one, nor the beautiful genius of the other, still like them both, I hope, she will try to live such a life only as woman should live, adorned by every virtue, and marred by no error. Brother must not think he has completed all of Parley's tales, because he has read one little book through. I do not know how many volumes there are, but they altogether make quite a library, and they contain a vast deal of excellent reading, both for old and young.

New-York Institution for the Blind.

Dear Cora:—The murmurs of the Genesee are in my thoughts to-night, and voices dear as home-words, have been falling on my ear, till I seem again surrounded by those who pitied and loved me long ago; whose homes were ever open for my reception, and their hands were never wearied with ministering to my wants.

The impressions of sound are much deeper and more lasting than those of sight, consequently the memories of the blind are always keepsakes of the heart. Another year has gone by, and I have yet no abiding place, save in the sympathies of friends—but like the wounded oyster who lines his shell with pearl, I would, by gentle love, make the dwellings I inhabit more pure and white. We cease to live when we have no longer something to do or bear; then why flee from ill, or pity those who suffer? Dews of the night are diamonds at morn, so the tears we weep here may be pearls in heaven; and we have little cause to mourn over the wreck of hopes, when it opens the heart to a brighter sunshine, whose warm light melts its ice to running streams, and covers its crags and cliffs with blossoms, and plants along its rough ways trees whose fruits and leaves are for the healing of the nations.

On Thanksgiving day, through the kindness of Mr. Dean, I heard Mr. ———. New-York has many eloquent men, but I have never heard one whose style is so richly beautiful, whose words are so select, and whose zeal seems so perfectly what the apostle calls according to knowledge. Tolerant towards all denominations, liberal in his views, more than cordial in his feelings, he seems to have a heart that could gather in all the world, and yet have room to spare.

I love such spirits; they are the lights of the age; beings whom heaven has destined "to leave foot-prints on the sands of time;" way-marks to all who would be wise, great, and good.

Mr. —— is but a few weeks home from Europe, and his imagery seems fresh as the sunny vales of England, grand as the glaciers of Switzerland, sublime as the scenery of the Rhine, clear and enrapturing as Italy's bowers where her time-honored painters drew, and where the sons of genius from all lands go to worship at the shrine of Art.

For a northern Thanksgiving dinner, roast turkey is always first in the bill of fare. My friend Mr. B——, with whom I dined, is a right true son of Johnny Bull as ever lived; whole-souled, whole-hearted, speaks always what he thinks, acts just as he feels, and his hospitality makes one as perfectly at home as himself. Mrs. B—— reminds me of what I once heard a Swede say of his countrywoman, Frederica Bremer; in the character of all persons, we ever find some one or more distinguishing trait, but in the soul of Frederica heaven has happily blended all excellence.

In the afternoon Mrs. B—— and I visited

the paintings at the Art Union; she was eyes for me, and beautifully described all she saw The most clever thing in the exhibition is the Mother's Prayer, which, while you gaze upon it, seems to breathe, as though touched by the pencil but now. I know not which to envy most, the purchaser or the artist, who, by the way, is an American. Another fine thing is the "Young Mechanic," by Mr. Smith, of Ohio; but perhaps the most famous work of all, is the "Voyage of Life," by Mr. Cole. The design is the Stream of Life, bearing on its rippled bosom a little boat, and in it an infant and an angel to guide. Farther on, the impetuous youth seats *himself* at the helm, dashes furiously on amidst rocks and breakers, so on down to tranquil old age, where all is calm and peaceful, and from the spirit-world which opens above, angels have come to beckon him away.

On our way from the gallery we chanced to pass the old Blind Harper, whose voice, like the strings of his worn harp, was trembling in the breeze; and while I listened to his sacred song, he seemed so like the weary pilgrim I had just heard described waiting on the boat, I almost fancied the angels above watching the close of his strain, to present him a new harp, tuned for ever to the praise of God and the Lamb. * * * *

At our last examination I met your friend Mr. G——, of Brooklyn, who is ever a welcome visitor at the New-York Institution for the Blind. His voice is a sort of watchword, at which the *little folks* quit their play, leave school and music, and run to greet him. Oh! could you see him once throw down his rolls and bundles filled with new dresses, &c., and to their infinite delight unburden his generous pockets of crackers, nuts, apples, and candies, some falling upon the floor, after which they all scramble, playing the kitten, as Mary says when she drops her ball, until they find them.

As the heavens are higher than the earth, so are God's ways above our ways; it is not the most useful who stay longest in the world, or to whom the power of doing good is longest preserved. Mr. G——, you are aware, is well known as a philanthropist, and a lover of mankind. No heart sympathizes more deeply with suffering than his, and no hand is open more readily and more widely to relieve it.

As the gifted Euler, in the Academy of Sciences in St. Petersburgh, saw his figures and angles fade, and all objects of sight pass into dim distance, so Mr. G—— tells me, the slow but sure hand of cataract is weaving her veils before his sight, which science has never reached and surgery has rarely turned away. Already the morning shines but dimly, the noon is painfully bright, the night shades are thick and foggy, his way is uncertain, and the faces of familiar friends look strangely, and not till they speak does he know one from the other. One hath said—

———— "to die is nothing,
But to live and not see is misfortune."

But it will not be so with Mr. G——. As Huber knew bees and their habits before his blindness, so Mr. G—— has learned the ways and the wants of the poor. And when the light shall cease to stream in upon his mind, the gladdened smile of the widow and orphan will be to his heart a sunshine, as pure and lasting as love in heaven. Adieu, Cora.

November, 1848.

Rochester, Carry's Home.

MY SCHOOL FRIEND LAURA :—It is pleasant to be even the sport of a chance breeze, while it continues to sit one down by pleasant places. You must know I have become a perfect wanderer ; claiming no abiding place with any sect, or people ; passing the time, however, always with the good, as invitations favor.

They tell me *gratitude*—that holiest of heavenly emotions—is too much the theme of my letters ; that I give words of thanks and praise to every body who is kind, all unmindful that green-eyed prejudice is still in the world. But, they who say thus should know, years have gone by since even a harsh word has fallen on my ears—since I have seen a frowning face, a look of anger or revenge. The cold, the unfeeling, whose souls are peopled with selfishness and haughty pride, never seek the friendship of the blind, but, like Priests and Levites, pass on the other side. So you see I am necessarily always with the good; for they alone find pleasure in contributing to the happiness of one, who can make no return for their multiplied favors. Miss Ferrier says beautifully in her "Marriage," "As the ancients held sacred the oak riven by the lightning, so a delicate mind always regards one who has been afflicted, as if touched by the hand of God himself."

We are creatures of habit, and form our notions of the world from what we *see* of it. Wonder not, then, if I call it only bright and beautiful. Those around may wear looks of sadness; may grow old; their teeth fall; their eyes become dim, and their locks gray; wrinkles may be on their brows, trace-marks of grief and care; but they look not so to me. The last time I saw the green earth, and its inhabitants, they wore yet the sunny hues of innocence and gladness, with which unsuspecting youth covers all things. And so they seem to me now; and were I to bear a report to heaven, I should call this a charming world, a kind, a loving, and a forgiving world; I should say men oftener love than hate, oftener do good than ill.

"Long, long be my heart with such memories filled,
Like the vase in which roses have once been distilled,
You may break, you may ruin the vase if you will,
But the scent of the roses will hang round it still."

It is Saturday, Laura, the preparation day of the Jews. A March morning, more lovely and clear, never graced an Italian sky. The ice-bands of the Genesee are broken, and its waters roll on, tossing liquid gems to the sunbeams. Robins, the first warblers among the leafless trees, are welcoming the Spring.

I have been with Lizzy and Carry to the place of prayer, and the solemnities of the house of God are still on my thoughts. White-haired age, and the young, were there, inquiring "what shall we do to be saved?" Mr. Wisner opened the exercises with the words, "Seek me early, and ye shall surely find me." Mr. Shaw followed, addressing himself most affectingly to the youth of his congregation; children of the Covenant. Miss Allen arose, and in tears, meekly asked the people of God to pray for the young ladies of her school, many of whom had accompanied her, seeking Jesus, whom to know aright is life eternal. "Blessed are the pure for they *shall* see God." This reminded me of like scenes in the old Seminary Chapel, where we so often assembled for prayers; when not *one* was left in the school who had not learned to pray and tasted that the Lord is good. The voices of those pious teachers, Professor Hoyt, Professor Whitlock, &c.; their lessons of instruction, their precious counsels, clustered around my heart, until it seemed "all life's scattered sweets were gathered into that one hour." Laura, now the sky is covered over with clouds, rain-drops are falling fast. Oh! that the dews of heavenly love, and the sweets of pardon, would so descend upon the earth, making it all like a well-watered garden, producing abundantly the fruits of righteousness.

As in nature, the brightest sunshine casts the deepest shadow, so human life is made up of contrasts of lights and shades, calms and storms, smiles and tears. Laura, we met amid scenes of mirth, we were happy, we were gay. We often met, and at every meeting gained something for our friendship's storage. You are still in the temple where we worshipped at the shrine of knowledge. The future is bright before you, and its symbols are big with joyous meaning. But, Laura, were I to ask a boon for thee, it would not be a life free from adverse winds and storms. Joy hath her ministers, but grief alone subdues and restrains the spirit. As the rod of the sainted Hebrew brought gushing waters from the rock, so sorrow moves the feeling fountains of the heart. While refreshing your mind at the springs of Castalia, forget not the once farewell words of our good Professor Seager, "First of all be Bible students." Ignorance of any thing else may be palliated, but if we lack knowledge of the Scriptures, we have no excuse, no pardon. Read often, then, the Word of God. It will add wisdom to your thoughts, peace to your life, and thereby good will come unto thee, and thy days shall be long upon the earth.

Friend Raymond:—I am again in New-York, the city of lights and fountains. Again in the Institution, that is real, that is true, but not sad.—Happiness does not so much depend upon circumstances as we think. Within our own hearts the fountain must well, else no number of tributaries can long keep alive its joyous gushings and laughing streams.

Our promenade grounds, in the rear of the Institution, covering several acres, are planted with trees from all quarters of the world, as are those who wander in their shade. The Ailanthus from China, the Catalpa from Japan, the silver-leaved Poplar and Abele from the South, the European Linden and Norway Fir, and the Maple and Elm from our own forests. The front yard is laid out with beautifully gravelled walks, and circles set round with shrubs and flowers. Our best of friends, Mr. Dean, who planted them, comes often to tell us of their beauties, their virtues and their native homes. But the old gardener, who has been servant in the Institution from first to last, when the flowers faded and the Autumn winds had strewed the ground with leaves, dead honors of the trees, the old man laid him down to die. No more he comes to teach our *truant feet* where not to tread, and our hands to find the fairest blossoms. He was a son of Erin, green isle of the sea ! and next his God, he loved his country. His history is to us all a mystery; but this we know, he had seen much of the world, knew much of men and manners. In his exile, books were his companions, and his well worn Bible still lies in the kitchen window, all unread and uncared for now.

The Croton is here, too, jetting its limeless waters in every part of the building; and the little boys say more birds come here to sing this summer than ever before; perhaps because the trees have grown thicker and higher. Prof. Root, the vocalist, sings with us two hours every morning.—Prof. Reiff, a German, who has for many years had entire control of the musical department, is with us still. If the consciousness of making others happy is earth's purest happiness, Professor Reiff must be blessed indeed. To how many of the Blind has he given employment, and made their hearts vibrate for ever with the melodies of song? Oh, could you hear him play once, you would think as I often do: he will have little cause for complaint if, up in heaven, the angels do not present him with a new harp, but let him keep his *old one.*

Miss Swetland, our preceptress, has returned from her tour South. Escaping the rigors of a northern winter has somewhat improved her health. Our leisure hours she beguiles with amusing incidents of her travels, visits to the Capitol, Mrs. Polk's levees, etc. Miss S. divided the winter months between Charleston and Washington, and as you may easily imagine, gathered much to interest those whose little world lies almost within these walls.

Last week, Gen. Scott and his Aids paid us a visit. The Band received him with "Hail to the Chief!" When passing them, the General took off his hat and bowed, which they unanimously returned. The members of the Band are all blind, and how knew they when to return his bow? Were not their spirits conscious of the deference a greater spirit was paying them? The soul immortal has eyes independent of the body, which like the quick spirits of the Universe, do neither sleep nor slumber, and no blindness can darken them. The particulars of the General's visit the public prints have already given you. Mr. Chamberlain, after introducing the great Hero, addressed him so beautifully in our behalf, that I must give you a copy of his words as nearly as I can recall them.

"Allow me, sir, on behalf of the managers, the officers and the pupils of this Institution, to bid you a cordial welcome. Although cut off from many sources of information enjoyed by our fellow-countrymen, with the history of your life, identified as it is with some of the brightest pages of our country's history, we are not unacquainted. All have heard of Fort Erie and of the Heights of Queenston; of the plains of Chippewa and of the sanguinary contest of Lundy's Lane. With our fingers we have traced the progress of that brave army, which from the storming of Vera Cruz to the capture of Mexico, you have led to triumph and to glory; and we have heard, too, that when "red field was won," and patriotism had sheathed her victorious sword, the claims of humanity were not forgotten. We have heard that the same heart which in the iron tempest of battle was firm as adamant, could dissolve in tenderest sympathy by the couch of the wounded and dying. All this, sir. we have heard, and while we have not admired the Hero less, we have loved the man more. It is for this, sir, that we cherish the name of Winfield Scott; one of the noblest names that fame has ever inscribed upon our national escutcheon;

'One of the few, the immortal names,
That were not born to die.'

"But I am reminded that of these precious moments very few can be accorded to us, and before we bid you adieu, I would crave one boon in behalf of my sightless charge. Some of these, when you shall have filled up the measure of your fame, and to you the praise and censure of man will be alike indifferent, will survive; and when they shall recount your achievements, and tell to coming generations, of Chippewa and of Cerro Gordo, and of Contreras, and the many other fields where you have covered the proud flag of our country with imperishable glory, I would have them say, too, that once, at least, it was their fortune to listen to the tones of that voice whose word of command was ever to the brave the talisman of assured victory."

Gen. Scott's reply was very concise and affecting. All his remarks I do not remember, but he said he knew by the light of our faces that our enjoyments, though perhaps more pensive than those of persons who see, are not less elevated and refined. Religion, God and the Bible were so much the themes of his remarks, one would sooner have thought him a priest, than a General from the field of battle. When he resumed his seat Fanny was introduced to him, and recited a poem which she had prepared for his reception. She alluded to the soldiers revelling in the halls of Montezuma. The General afterwards remarked: "we did not revel in the Halls of Montezuma, but subsisted on one meal a day; and when the battle ended went down on our knees, as all good Christians and soldiers should do, and returned thanks, and sought the blessing of God." If analyzed, were their thanks for their own escape, or for their success in disposing of their enemies? Even soldiers should remember, "God takes no thanks for murder." The General let Fanny take his sword; she unsheathed it, and raising it high, exclaimed, "You are my prisoner." The great man replied, "I always surrender to the ladies at discretion." He then joked her something about the beaux. Fanny said to him, I have never yet *seen* a gentleman who *quite* suited my fancy. This put the house in a roar of laughter, and such a volley of cheers you never heard. I could not see the General to judge of his height, but I fancy he must be to the new world what Saul was to the old, "head and shoulders above all other men."

Rochester Willow Bank, March, 1848.

MY DEAR, VERY DEAR MARY:—We, whose eyes are closed, have but two divisions of time —a noisy night and a quiet one. Morning comes, and the light streams in sunny rills over all the gladsome earth. Long ago, Mary, we two awoke, ere the sun had kissed the dews into vapor, and ran joyous to greet the faces of those we loved, refreshed and beautified by a night of slumbers. And oh, do you remember, Mary, how from the opened doors, in rushed, like resisted waters, a flood of golden light? When far o'er the green hills, the full orbed sun showered his splendors; and high up the blue sky, fleecy clouds were flying; and among the trees merry birds were singing— and on the flowers, busy bees their nectar draughts were sipping, and all the insect tribes were humming, and we, too, in girlhood glee, went singing. How joyful, oh, how joyful, is the morning! But now it is not so; *our* night is unending. Days steal on us—and steal from us. We sleep and awaken; but no change comes. No flowers spring up in our path; no garden walks or fields unfold their colors; no mountains rise—no rivers roll nor oceans swell. To *us*, beauty hath veiled her face, and grandeur and sublimity, have passed away. Yes, Mary, all things have passed away. The moon has left the sky, and all the constellated stars have gone down for ever; so the bright dreams of our youth have fled; and promised joys come not. All around are blithe and gay, but from morn till eve, Mary, we move cautiously and pensively. Our truant feet often go astray, and we know not when danger is nigh. As the chained eaglet looks heavenward, and stretches out its wing in fancied freedom, so we sometimes intercept the flight of time—and live forgetful in light, and joy, and hope, only to return and weep in darkness *more* dark, and loneliness *more* lonely. But Mary, our darkness, like the clouds, must have its sunny side, for God takes blessings from us only when their absence is the greater blessing; sorrow sanctified, quickens into newness of life, the better feelings of our nature,—and Mary, does it not make us love our friends and all the world more; and go not our thoughts oftener up to God and heaven? Imagination, that sublime radius of the soul, is every day taking to herself a broader sweep; piercing even the sepulchre of the buried past—and treading fearless, within the boundary of the unseen. Science or art, or earth or sky, have no treasured worth, nor hidden beauty, that fancy, in her fleetness, does not picture in colors brighter far, than open eyes can see; and as flowers from the depths of the ocean, come floating o'er the swelling tide, so beautiful images from the long-forgotten past, gladden now our searching memories. Galileo, who saw more than all the world before him, and opened the eyes of all after him, from the top of his prison, with the instrument his own hands had made, watched the wheeling orbs above, until his eyes became opaque as the satellites he discovered; in his woes he cried, Oh, ye Gods, for power to look once more into the serene depths of the clear night heaven! If we may judge from his frequent and happy descriptions of its beauties, Milton would have given all other sights for the glorious morning.

Sanderson desired only once to look along the pages of a book, and I have heard you say Mary, you would rather see the flowers, than all the world beside! But oh! if I were to be blessed with one moment of sight, I would pray, let me look again into the face of a cherished friend—a pair of soul-lit eyes, beaming with intelligence and love; whose spirit-glances imagination cannot picture, and things so holy, unsanctified memory may not treasure. Oh, what saddened feelings steal upon us, when, with ravished ears, we listen to descriptions of paintings on the walls, and rainbows on the clouds. But, Mary, have you never thought the angels are always nearer then, to bear our thoughts away, where light is, that fades not? Where the painter, with his brush of divine art, dipped in color's native well, sketches holy imagery; scenery of heaven, where deathless flowers bloom by living fountains, and the fair forms of the blest, when dayspring's fragrant dews hang impearled upon their seraph locks! Where the poet, seated upon some blissfu mound, writes while the inspirations of holy genius burn along his lines, where Truths, into which philosophers here look and grow bewildered with their depth, we shall there explore, invited by the voice of Him who sits in majesty enthroned, and sways over earth and heaven his potent rule; whose creating hand moulds worlds, and tosses them into the fields of ether pensile hung; "clothes the lilies of the field, and tempers the winds to the shorn lamb."

Mary, life is what we make it; shut out from all that is external, we are pretty much the creators of the world we live in. Let us see to it then, that we be good creators. Since day and night are the same, we can as well people our minds with the beams of the one, as the clouds of the other; as well call back images of joy and gladness, as those of grief and care. The latter, however, may sometimes be our guests to sup and dine, but let them never be permitted to lodge with us. We came forth in childhood's morn to gather flowers, and because on our way we have dropped a few, we will not sit down and weep over the lost, but rather amuse ourselves by counting and admiring those we have left.

Blindness makes us painfully dependent; but God forbid our hearts murmur, or our lips complain. "The earth is the Lord's and the fulness thereof." The cattle upon a thousand hills are his; running waters and green pastures are in his hands, and even now, he may be leading us *hither*, by ways we have not known! In the love and sympathy of friends, who every where hasten to do us kindness, we have a well-spring of pleasure, inexhaustible as the good feelings of the human heart. Cora is an angel of patience, Mary, or I had not written you so long a letter. Her little hand must be weary, though she says no, and when I complain of troubling her, she folds her arms around my neck and whispers, afflicted friends are our ministering spirits—for us they languish—for us they die.

Mary, it is four by the clock, and I fancy myself again in the Institution parlor, drumming a piano lesson, as if noise were its only object. Now opens the door; Kitty, Libby, Josey, and Susa, all in the same breath inquire, Mr. Dean? Mr. Dean? No; he has not come yet; away they run and presently return with some dozen more; now they are not mistaken; his well-known tread in the hall they heard, and his voice guides them to his arms; some are in his lap, others hang around his chair; all expect a kiss, a kind word; yes, and something more.—Look! what has he now for these, his pet children? Pine-apples, bananas, figs, oranges! These with a father's fondness he divides, answering meantime their many questions of the people who grow and gather such delicious fruits; how preserved, where procured, &c.—But where is Charley, the pet of all the house? forgive the little rogue, he has gone trudging up the long stairs with a heart full of complaint to Miss Wild, that his apron-pockets ain't "*bigger enough.*" Patting them on the head affectionately, Mr. Dean says, go away now my children to your play, while I read a little to these larger girls; bless his heart! some choice book we know, perhaps just from the press; and as we sit encircled round, hour after hour goes unheeded by, till late in the evening we bid him good night at the yard gate. It is a long walk to Mr. Dean's mansion, but happy thoughts, like good society, always annihilate time and distance. Oh! Mary, is it not heart-mending to live over in after time, seasons of such rich enjoyment. I often wonder who comes to read for you on Sabbath evenings, now our friend Mr. Murray has made his home in Oswego. We never forget those to whom we have been truly kind; so we will hope thoughts of those whom his frequent visits made so happy, will come to him sometimes even there. Yesterday, two Canaries were presented me; one I shall bring to you, and the other to Ann. Their voices are equalled in sweetness by none but your own. Pardon me, if I flatter, but I could not compliment their musical powers more, or describe them to you better.—Remember me kindly to all in the Institution, and say, in the month of roses I shall again be with them. Good-by, Mary.

New-York Institution for the Blind.

FRIEND CARRIE,—In the light of many memories I sit me down to write you. The holidays came, and all were again abroad for a little season of pleasure, and I need not tell you that the Institution began to seem lonely enough, to those too far from home and friends to share with them the recreations of the season; when to my delight Mr. H. M. Whitney, of Rochester, came and escorted me over to Brooklyn. The old Dutch custom of devoting the first day of the New Year exclusively to calling, for the gentlemen, is still kept up with much enthusiasm in New-York and Brooklyn. For this one day in the year at least, the ladies do turn democrats, and with open doors and hearts receive with free toleration, all those who choose to look in upon them. It is a nice way too of adding new acquaintances to one's list; for instance, if there chance to be a strange family in the neighborhood, or church, and a gentleman, by introduction or otherwise, pays the lady a New Year's call, she soon after, if the acquaintance be a desirable one, returns the obligation by calling at his house.

There was never a brighter winter morning than dawned with the new year. Broadway was one grand masquerade. Proteus had less shapes than the fashions of its equipage.

Heads of buffaloes, bears, lions, and tigers, were mounted on every stage-coach, omnibus, and all sorts of vehicles that go on wheels or runners. I do not mean that these creatures were really abroad so uncaged, but lesser animals, you know, sometimes wrap themselves in the skin of the stronger, and go about like the sheep in wolf's clothing.

Among the many who called on my friends Mrs. Barnes and her sister, was the learned Professor Davies. Mathematicians are not always social in their feelings, fertile in imagination, or fluent in speech; but I have seldom met so cordial, warm-hearted, and happy man in conversation, as Professor Davies. Listening to him, you would think he numbers all the *fine arts* in his string, and his *formulas* and *infinite series* besides. By some association, the cause of my blindness was asked; whereupon I told the good Professor plainly, that I believed *he* had something to do with it; that I strove too hard to see the end of his mathematical course, and after passing many wearisome days and nights with his too fascinating Legendre, Bourdon, surveying, and calculus of radicals, an irritation by weeping and a slight cold darkened my eyes for ever. Now, Carrie, if I could only manage to demonstrate to the Professor, by one of his own formulas, that he was, in point of fact, the original cause of my blindness, I see no reason why I should not send in my bill to him; and how much should it be? Really, one could not think of asking less than a thousand dollars for a pair of hazel orbs, such as mine were, always bright with looks of gladness, to say nothing of their usefulness; and that sum, Carrie, would make me independently rich,—for you must know, since Mr. Dean sent me to the water-cure establishment, I have learned to live without meat, butter, salt, tea or coffee; quenching my thirst always, as Kirke White says, "luxurious from the limpid wave." And according to Graham's computation, a true vegetarian can fare sumptuously as need be upon fifteen dollars per year; and, certainly, the difference between that and seventy would clothe one, and pocket money beside. God grant that little fortune may yet be mine; then I shall be the happiest creature alive.

Well, we had other calls, too; the gallant, the brave, the young, the gifted, and fascinating, all pouring in pell-mell, by the score and dozens, with a "happy New Year" on their lips, music in their voices, and their brows clothed with smiles, new from the fair faces they had just left.

It is astonishing how many words and ideas can be exchanged in a little time when both parties are agreeably excited. Seemingly, in five minutes, Dr. Powers gave us a synopsis of the different modes of observing the day in all the countries of Europe. The polished Marquand introduced us to Paris scenes so familiarly, that we seemed almost enjoying her dazzling fêtes. Mr. Humphrey, of Amherst, talked of paintings, then the classics, the land of marvels, and our genius, Powers, in Florence; and lastly, reference was made to the New England festival, where I believe he was toasted "orator of the day." Lawyer Burr had on his sunniest face; though emphatically a man of the world, a calculating and speculative disciple of Blackstone, yet no laugh was so merry as his, and no efforts to please more heartfelt. I envy you such an uncle; and why should I not? Just think of his holiday gifts; Mrs. B——'s hundred dollar ring, and Emma's pearl and feather fan, and splendid books beside.

Sunday morning we went to the Mission Sunday School, the children of which are gathered from the highways and hedges. Could you see these little ones in their cellar homes, and contrast them now in the cheerful Sunday School. The hand of benevolence has washed them from their filth, put on them comely garments, and set their feet in new shoes, and while I listened to them repeating the A, B, C, and reading stammeringly, verses of Scripture, they seemed a cabinet of unwrought jewels, and every lesson a touch from the hand of the polisher, revealing some new and heavenly beauty. The school at present numbers one hundred and fifty-seven, taught and sustained by those of all denominations, who, like the great Teacher of mankind, love to do good. Mr. Barnes, for a New Year's gift, presented each of them, one of Mrs. Sherwood's stories for children. Poverty is a school, but her discipline is not always healthful to the mind and heart; too often her children become proficients in art and deceit, which they through life practise upon an unsuspecting world. Even there a child, too provident, was found smuggling a second book to sell on the morrow, as she said, for a penny to buy bread. Children can be drawn and kept in the right way only by the cord of love, and their waywardness should be checked by the same. My lips will never cease to whisper blessings on the members of the Mission Sunday School; and may God love and bless them too.

Friend Carrie, believe always, that I love you. With the compliments and good wishes of the season,

I am affectionately yours.

Institution for the Blind.

MANY things are dark to sorrow, but not all; even blindness has its morning and its evening.—True, at night we cannot see the stars in their blue homes, nor the sun at morn;

yet they both have many voices, and when the eye is turned away, the ear affords new avenues to the heart, through which the spirit, though a prisoner, may become elevated and happy.

New-York Institution for the Blind seems a paradise, where purity dwells, peace and content rule all hearts, and love is our guardian angel.—The murmur of the Hudson blends with the breeze, and high in the new-leafed trees birds sing the hours away. It is a home of flowers, where blind girls wander in angel innocence, now twining garlands in their hair, now bowing their heads to smell and kiss the blossoms, they may not pluck; and with thankful lips they speak of him who placed them there.

The sun has veiled his splendors behind the hills, save here and there a truant beam lingering, as if reluctant to quit the world, till *my poor eyes* have seen their light. School duties are over, all are abroad, each to his favorite diversion. Eddy, the blind Pole, (better known as the blind prodigy,) is at the organ. Haydn's Creation is now a creation of his own.

The spirit of its author is on him; he is the personation of genius; the sightless spirit of lovely sounds. Here comes my little friend Cynthia, the blind poetess, to tend her plants. Whispers are on her lips low and sweet as angel lutes; her thoughts go in rhymes. A copy of her Poems has lately been published, a thank-offering to her friends, which like herself, every where meets a warm reception.

Now the air all around rings with the school-girl's merry laugh—the old servant who has been in the Institution since it was founded, from years and respect has long had the title of Mr.———, is with them at the swing. "Ride fareless, my pretty craturs," says he, "and if the swang comes down, I'll be after catching your swate souls, all in my arms, to be sure."

A school like this is a world by itself, the manners and customs of which are as unlike the real world as possible. A few evenings since, I chanced to be in the little girls' sitting-room; the subject of their innocent conversation, then happened to be, the birds. "The Canary is the sweetest singer in the world," says Cassy. "That may be," says Lizzy, "but its feathers are not half so soft and pretty as the grasshopper's." "Psha," says one more experienced, "the grasshopper is not a bird." "It is," says Lizzy; "I have felt them fly against my head, many a time, though my little hands could never catch one; and sister Mary used to say they were a beautiful green, and she wished I could see them."

Another time little Matta says to Angy, "Do you know that, when you speak a lie, the guilty feeling comes out all over your face, so that those who see you know that you are telling a story?" "No," says Angy, "I do not think it, though I have heard mamma say to little brother, You are guilty, I can see it in your eyes; and you know my eyes are closed, and she never said so to me." "Well, it is so," says Matta, "and that is the way God sees our hearts, and knows all we are thinking."

The past and the present are as the two sides to a pane of glass—we cannot see the one, without seeing the other; now, I remember the morning when Mr. Loder left me here.

In Rochester I was always surrounded by the best of friends, by whom my every wish was anticipated; but here it was not so, and more than ever I felt that I was blind and in the world alone. Two long days wore away—then came the Sabbath—and a Sabbath in a strange land is a lonely day indeed; during the morning service, I heard nothing. My thoughts were far away over the current of years—my soul turned back upon itself, and in my heart I said; "to die is nothing, but to live and not see, is misfortune." When all had left the Chapel but myself, I began groping my way back to the parlor. There all were social and happy, as mortals may be, but my heart was too full for words or tears.

Presently a tread was heard inside the door; "Oh! Mr. Dean, Mr. Dean," exclaimed every voice, "have you come? we are glad to see you. Have you brought a book? what is it? and how long will you read to us?" Mr. Dean is one of the Managers, and a kind father to us all; and though a man of business and his residence in town, yet he finds time to visit us every day, and the interviews are to us all lights in a dark place. In a few days he brought his daughter to see me, to whose kindness I owe much happiness. Her friendship has been to me what Mungo Park's flower was to him in the Desert.

After seven months' confinement to the walls of an Institution, can you imagine with what transport I received through her an invitation to pass a little time in the family of Mrs. Allen, of Newark, New Jersey, the city of Elms. Her home is "seated soft among the trees." Mrs. A. has seen many years; her heart is the home of pious emotions, and to know her is to love her.

Not long since, through the kindness of Mr. Townsend, of this city, I had the pleasure of hearing Dr. Dewey, who has lately returned from Washington. I had heard the remark that he was not so eloquent in the pulpit as with his pen; that, like Goldsmith, he could reason best when alone; but a more eloquent and heart-healing discourse I have seldom heard. In consequence of declining health, he is about closing his ministerial labors and works of love; but he will leave with his people a name set round with good deeds, like a diadem of honor. * * * * *

Institution for the Blind.

MY EVER DEAR ELIZA:—I planted you in my heart long ago; it was then a garden plot, fresh and green, and full of blossoms. But now, how changed! Mildew and death are there, and frosts cold and frigid have turned its leaves, and sleety winds have shaken them to the ground. And yet, dearest, you stand now as then, firm and beautiful. Like the oak, you have spread your branches, and I in my weariness come to repose in their shade.

Eliza, many times the moon has waned since I wrote to you; but loving as her beams on the hills, are my memories of the Seneca, and those who dwell by its shore. I have been ill. Health is indeed a precious gift, without it we can hardly be happy within ourselves, or useful to those around us. Suffering the will of God, and doing it, are very unlike; but in every condition we have something to be grateful for. Indeed, I doubt, if we are ever so placed that we have not more smiles for the day, than tears for the night, and more cause for joy than mourning. Watchful spirits are at every post. Angels with folded pinions are in every path, indeed the world is full of them. Our feet never stumble, want never approaches, and ills of any kind are seldom long in the way, but some Samaritan hand lifts us out of them. No night is so dark that our Father's smile cannot cheer it, and no place is so barren, so far removed, that his blessings and mercies cannot reach it. And how rich and bountiful they come. New every morning, fresh every evening, and repeated every moment of our lives.

It is November. The frost has bitten the forest leaves, and the trees are robed in Autumn's bleeding hues. The day-god is in the sky, gladdening all the world, but oh, he sheds no light for me. Nothing strikes the chord of responsive memories like music. Eliza, this morning the Band are in the chapel, playing Love Not, and the variations; and without the winds are blowing a sort of trumpet accompaniment; now, the tide of their rich harmony ebbs and flows along the borders of my soul, kindling my thoughts, and making my pulses beat quicker. Now they are scattering Mozart's Requiem on the air. Oh, Heaven be always thanked for an atmosphere that may be formed into sweet sounds. Looks of love are bright things, but words are far more dear. The former play upon the heart like moonbeams upon the waters, but the latter sink down into it, thence coming forth in blossoms and clustering fruits, like seeds lost in the earth. No wonder the deaf Beethoven by *gesturing words* exclaimed, "all the pleasures of sight and sense, all my eyes ever saw, would I give for one whisper to my heart."

Rochester, *Oct.*, 1846.

DEAR CLARA:—'Tis Autumn, and to-day the winds howl mournfully among the trees. Four long weeks I have been pillowed on a sick couch, and though with much of its drapery around me, I can to-day sit in an easy chair. Fever still burns on my cheeks, and my brow is pressed with throbbing pain. Last night they fed me opium, and I slept a pleasant sleep. I dreamed of other days. I thought that we again, arm in arm, paced the halls of the old seminary, and talked confidingly of bright realities in the future. The chime of the welcome school-bell again rang in my ears, and I heard the halls echo with the familiar tread of many feet, and mingling voices, all buoyant with hope and love.

This morning I engaged a friend to write for me, while I fancy myself whispering in your ear the story of all that grieves me, and wrings every joy from my heart. "Truth is often stranger than fiction," and the tale I shall tell you needs no coloring. Clara, *I am blind!* for ever shrouded in the thick darkness of an endless night. And now, when I look down the current of coming years, a heavy gloom settles on me, almost to suffocation. Is there any sympathy in your heart? Oh then weep with me, for now, like an obstinate prisoner, I feel my spirit struggling to be free. But oh, 'tis all in vain, 'tis all over, misery's self seems stopping my breath, hope is dead, and my heart sinks within me. Clara, I am in a land of strangers too. Stranger voices sound in my ears, and stranger hands smooth my brow, and administer to my wants. I see them not, but I know they have learned the laws of kindness. I love them, and pray Heaven to hold them in remembrance.

But let me change the subject. The first year after we parted at school, my love of knowledge increased every day. I continued Italian with a success that pleased me. I read various French authors, besides translating most of the Old Testament Scriptures, reviewed Rollin, &c.

In June last, Dr. De Kroyft was seized with hemorrhage of the lungs. He sent for me and I came to him. Every day his lips grew whiter, and the deep paleness on his brow alarmed me. Now, in a half-coughing tone, I hear him say, Helen, I fear the hand of consumption is settling on me, and my days will soon be numbered. On the afternoon of the Fourth he visited me, went out, and returned no more. Our wedding-day came. It was his wish, and by his bedside our marriage was confirmed. Soon after I saw him die. They laid him in the ground, and I heard the fresh dirt rattle on his narrow home, and felt as if my hold on life had left me. I lingered in R—— a little time longer. How I got through the days I do not know. William's room, his books, and the garden where I wept, are all I remember, until I awoke one morning and my eyes were swollen tight together. I could no more move them, or lift up the lids, than roll the mountains from their places. They were swollen with an inflammation that three days after made me for ever blind—oh, the word! Like the thunders of Niagara it was more than I could hear. Thus, dear Clara, in simplicity, I have told you all. No, not the half. Words can never reach the feelings that swell my heart, imagination can never paint them. They are known only to me. Sorrow, melancholy, blighted hopes, wounded love, grief and despair, clad in hues of darkness, all brood upon my silent heart, and bitter fear is in all my thoughts. Oh, what will become of me? Is there benevolence in this world? Must charity supply my wants? Will there be always some hand to lead me? Have the blind ever a home in any heart? Does any thing ever cheer them? Are their lives always useless? Is there any thing they can do? So I question, and wonder, until with morphine they quiet my distracted thoughts. When my eyes were swelling as if they would quit their sockets, and my entire being was racked with pain, forgive me, Clara, I did question if there be a God in heaven who is always merciful. But to-day, in the calmness of better feelings, my confidence is unmoved, and "though he slay me, yet will I trust in him." Though I do not feel all the self-abnegation of Fenelon, yet I am certain my heavenly Father loves me, and will grant me ever his protecting care and sustaining grace. Adieu, but think of me, and pray for me sometimes.

P. S. Dear Clara:—This is the first letter I have prompted to any one, and is it possible that I am never again to write with my own hand, or read the letters of my friends when they come? Oh God! save me, lest I murmur. You must write my dear mother, Clara, and comfort her, for I cannot. * * * * *

Institution for the Blind.

Dear Eliza:—To-morrow you will leave school, you say, to return "never more." Solemn words. When our lovely parent Eve made her last round of delight in her garden home, played gently with her sportive fawns, pressed kisses on her flowers, and lingered by Eden's meandering streams, whose murmurs seemed a lower strain, blending sweetly with the songs of her caressing birds, she smiled sadly on all she loved, and passing hurriedly the closing gate, the words of the protecting Angel fell on her ear—"Never more!" "never more!" They went on, Adam and Eve, beautiful though fallen; thorns grew up in their paths, but memory, ever wont to dwell on what is pleasing, often reverted to lovely Eden, its laughing brooks and fountains, where seraphs had been their familiar guests; but

Eve could only sigh "never more!" The winds and the zephyrs caught the melancholy air, and to the farthest verge of time echo's last response will be—"Never more," "never more." When first the fountain of a mother's feelings was stirred, looking despairingly on the form of her child, cold in death, the Angels beheld what till then they had never seen, a spirit or mortal weeping for that which may return, never more. Tears are the language of feeling, the dews that water love, and keep it alive when its leaves would wither.

Eliza, believe me, it is better that you learn early what hardships are, and how to meet life's many ills. Begin now to share another's woe, and help to bear the burden under which thy neighbor may be sinking. Check often thy mirth and go to the house of mourning, and school thy buoyant voice to speak soothingly to the distressed. Life is not a dream. Young or old, we have always something to do, and something to bear. Our work too is here, and the voice of beseeching suffering calls us to it, and the cry of love and philanthropy is, "Come over and help us." Fields of usefulness are as many as the doors which enter the abodes of the poor. And have *you* nothing to do? Shall your hands be busy only to adorn your frail body and twine garlands of flowers? Have you no energies of heart and mind to spend in the great work of self-culture, and the amelioration of mankind? The terms you have passed at school, have enriched your heart with enlightened feelings, and stored your mind with new and aspiring thoughts; you have received new impulses to your progressive nature, and enlargement of your mental and moral capacities, for which you are answerable, and will be held responsible to the great Father of mankind. The philanthropic Howard, speaking of a young friend, said, "She taught me to forget myself and live for my neighbor." Her morning and evening visits to the poor were simple in themselves, but in their effects you see they were boundless and lasting as eternity. When Henry Martin's sister hung affectionately about his neck, entreating him with all the earnestness of tears to remain with her, he replied: "Sister, the Saviour you taught me to love has a work for me in a heathen land, and I shall go to it, trusting your prayers and His love will sustain me there." Such homebound efforts and examples are swelling springs in the hillside, whence flow multiplying and fertilizing streams, whose healthful influences are felt throughout the world. They are seeds planted here to blossom in a higher, holier life. Now while you are lingering on ground so hallowed, so sacred to the heart and memory of both teacher and scholar, would that some heaven-born resolve, worthy the place and the hour, might find a lodgment in your thoughts, and a resting place in your heart. It is the misfortune of some to be ever vacillating between good purposes and their non-performance. If you would be truly useful, continued and persevering action must mark your every course. Take unto thyself then a standard of what is right, and make all else yield thereunto. Then, what though thy smiles fade and tears come in their stead, and the world frown darkly on thee, if so there be no clouds between thee and thy God?

Brooklyn, Anniversary Week.

FRIEND CARRY:—The last six months I have drummed a piano at the rate of seven hours per day. And now, when I see how little I have acquired that is really useful, I am ready to exclaim with Mrs. Hopkins' cook, "Oh! what an inglorious way of spending one's time!" Music is indeed a science of difficult attainment, and in order to excel, even the most gifted must commence it in early life. For however well one may understand the theory, *manual skill* is wanting.

* * * * *

The British bard was not far from right when he said "in life there is no present;" for certainly a moment is no sooner here, than it is gone, and we find ourselves either drawing from the past, or robbing an imagined future. Remind you, dear, of mornings in the old seminary, when your room-mate, Helen, returned from a recitation, and in girlish glee tossed her books upon the table, and perchance shook you until the tasteful braids of your hair tumbled down, and then, to make all well, kissed your lips, and promised never to do the like again. Carry, as I loved you then, I love you now. Care has left some traces upon my brow, but really the order of my feelings is but little changed. Perhaps I am wrong, but I always allow myself to think the fault is in the place instead of my eyes, and persuade myself I should see well enough if the blinds were only thrown open, or the lights brought in. But it is not so; the windows of my soul are surely darkened, and no light is there, save the unborrowed lustre of its own jewels, and the mingled rays of those spirit stars, love and hope, which never set. Cheered by their light, Milton wove his celestial strains, Gough pursued his botany, culled his flowers, and arranged his plants; the Swiss Huber tended his bees, Buret chiselled marble, and Giovanni Gonelli moulded clay into forms that to their gentle touch seemed warming into life.

I wonder if St. Paul was blind. I believe Hannah More in her beautiful essay upon him, thinks he was. If so, he must have managed to write better than I do, or there was no need of his explaining to the Corinthians, that he had saluted them with his own hand.

Mr. Crittenden has removed from Albany, and presides in the Brooklyn Female Academy Yesterday I attended his anniversary examination. I thought the recitations more systematic and thorough than any I have ever heard from classes composed only of ladies.

Besides, I like Mr. C.'s mode of examining; he only names the subject, without any assisting interrogatories. The pupil is then required to follow closely the reasonings of the author, giving his ideas in her own words.

The recitations were mostly heard in the library, and during the interim of classes Miss Emily gave me its etceteras. In the middle of the floor is a large case of birds, gracefully perched, but voiceless as they are lifeless. The books are new, and mostly from modern and select authors. The cabinets are quite large, but the chemical and philosophical apparatus is yet in its infancy, though they say it is growing fast. The picture gallery is an upper room, lighted from the sky. The walls are covered with pencillings and paintings of the young ladies. It is customary for each to leave there a piece of her work. There is something in this idea exceedingly pleasing to me. There stood their easels with half-finished paintings on them; "ekes of men and women," as Kirke White says; and half-drawn rivers, and outlined ruins of cities and castles. Last evening we heard Strakosch again, the celebrated pianist to the Emperor Nicholas. I wish you could once hear his fingers dance through the mazes of sound, almost up to the highest note in all nature, which Professor Whitlock says is the noise the musquito makes when he beats the air with his wings; then down to the low flutter of the miller, and the far-off droppings of falling water. His style is so fascinating, dear me! if all the Emperor's subjects are like him, I envy him his reign. Why it would be like sitting upon the summit of delight, with harping fairies at one's feet. Have you read Mr. Jacob Abbot's "Crowned Heads of Europe?" Not long since I passed a day in his school Being near the close of the term, the young ladies were exchanging parting gifts. One received a Chinese work-box, and gave in return a beautiful guitar, and a volume of Jenny Lind's songs,—paintings, books, boxes, card-cases, bracelets, rings, daguerreotypes, &c., were among their tokens of school-day love. About the whole establishment there seemed an air of wealth and refinement. Mr. Abbot was exceedingly affable ; he spoke very freely of his travels, books, &c. When some reference was had to the great excellence of his productions, he very modestly replied, "I only wish they were better." Carry, I purposed writing you only a little note, but really I have made quite a letter of it, if indeed the stringing together of disjointed sentences can in any case make a letter.

Friend Phin:—Not more welcome could be the appearance of an *Inn* to a weary traveller, than was your kind letter to me. It came when it so happened that most of our *seeing* people were absent, and with it in hand, I ran many times from first to third story, dodging in at every door, in pursuit of a *pair*

5*

of eyes. At length an old servant, by aid of his glasses, spelled out the name upon the margin, and my curiosity thus much relieved, I went on with my practising. We have no such thing here as music with raised notes. We are all taught orally, and play from memory, the same as I would have learned music elsewhere, only perhaps more scientifically. I find the blind folks here a singular sort of people indeed. Their habits, manners, and ideas of things are so unlike *the world*, that "I am to them all a foreigner," as the Paddy said of the French. * * * * Now Phin, you are not far from right when you call this Institution a *nunnery*, for it is certainly a place where ladies retire from the world, and never more *see* the face of man. Some are here for life; others for a specified time. We have nine pianos in the Institution, and some eighty who practise upon them, which affords only one hour each per day. We have also two organs, besides violins, flutes, and a large brass band. All these going, I quite forget I am inclosed with iron doors, and granite walls, and seem the inhabitant of a spirit land, where harmony reigns, anthems are ever new, and "ever throbs with melody the air."

I wish you would come over some time, and take a run with us around the gymnastic pole, a walk on the promenade grounds, or a swing in what they call the *scupp*. I pass an hour every morning in the upper piazza, on the side of the building that looks away towards Rochester. Oh truly, the fairest land is where our friends abide. Rochester has been to me an eventful place. There my eyes first opened to this beautiful world, and there they closed upon its glories for ever. There I learned to love, and there I breathed love's vows; there I saw the guardian angel break the idol of my affections; there, in the night-time of sorrow and care, strangers took me up, and blessed me, and loved me too. Oh chide me not then, if, more than all the world beside, I love the warm hearts of Rochester.

Stone Cottage.

The stars are bright on the brook by the door, as if they had alighted there, awhile to bathe and watch their shadows in the sky whence they came. Night, oh lovely night; in thy peaceful hours the heart is ever wont to go abroad in search of those it holds most dear. The last hour, Nin has been reading me "The Lays of Many Hours," by Miss Maylin, of Salem, New Jersey, a cousin of the distinguished Dr. Bowring, of England: there is a beautiful ease in the tread of her fancies, which reminds me of Mrs. Embury.

Yesterday we finished "The Neighbors," and in the evening paper saw a notice, that its fair authoress is on her way to our country. I wonder who will go out to meet her. Certainly, the ladies of our land should do something to signalize their gratitude and esteem for one of their sisters, from whom they have received so many lessons of literary and domestic instruction. * * * *

Nine summers ago, in a neat school-room, a

little way down the hill from my uncle's, I played the school-mistress. One day, a black-eyed, curly-headed little boy, with a green satchel on his arm and a straw hat in his hand, walked into the room and accosted me so handsomely, that I was straightway in love with him; and when I asked his name, he replied promptly, "Master William Lovejoy, Ma'am; my father and mother are travelling this summer, and if you please, they have sent me to attend your school." "Ah!" said I, we are indeed very happy to welcome you one of our little number." Then by way of attention, I gave him a conspicuous seat, hung up his hat, then opened his satchel and looked over his books, smoothed down his curls, and patted his rosy cheeks, until the new-comer seemed to feel himself quite at home; then I went on again hearing my little ones read their a, b, c, and spell out their b l a, bla! But ever and anon my eyes wandered to little William's seat; and as often met *his*, glancing over his shoulder, peeping quizzingly into the face of one, and exchanging knowing looks with another, and when he saw me observing him, half laughed, and looked on his book again.

I soon learned that his mother was a distant relative of my aunt, which served not a little to increase the interest I already felt in my new pupil. However, the summer wore away, the school closed, William's parents returned and took him to their home. Another summer passed, and my dear aunt died. I saw them lay her in the grave; and shortly after William's mother came to me, saying, "Evermore I will be your aunt, and my home shall be your home." And his father added, "Yes; and if she will be a good girl, she may have me for her uncle;" "and me for Cousin Will," shouted a sweet voice, and with his arms around my neck, half said and half kissed Cousin Helen, on my tearful cheek.

A few years after, when these rayless shades had but lately gathered about me, a letter from Cousin Will first broke my melancholy.—"Come to us," said he; "we think of you all the time. Come, do come soon; bring all your books and every thing. Mother and I have made all the plans for the winter—what we shall read, and where we shall go, and so on. Your pet table has been in my room this summer, and that old chair with the squeaking back you loved so well; but they are all replaced now, and it looks there again as if my dear coz. had but just stepped out." * * *

Friday, you know, was our National Fast Day. I took no supper the previous evening, nor breakfast the next morning; attended church at St. Luke's; heard Marion play. During the service I took it into my head and heart to be lonely, and on my way home said to sister, "Come, let us go and see what time the stage leaves for F." In spite of her remonstrances we did so, and at three I took a seat for a ride of twelve miles, over to the home of my black-eyed, curly-headed Cousin Will. There all my books and papers were, and all my letters since I first began to write, and all the little relics of my school-days, which Cousin Will read for me, and I tore them in pieces and burned them. Not a scrap have I left which has my handwriting on it, save a little French song which I copied a long time ago. That I preserved for you, and a drawing of a little tired deer crawled among the brambles to die. In my Bible I found a book-mark which I send you, for my hands will do those things no more.

Many days Cousin Will and I have wandered together in the woods, and under the old elm tree, a little back of the house, read poetry hours together, until his speaking eyes saw beauty in every thing. Now, we wandered over the same grounds, he guiding me, where long ago I led him. * * * * *

Long Island, Water Cure, Aug. 30, 1848.

It was a chance breeze that blew us together, and Monday morning the same bore us apart. We met as strangers always meet, but our spirits came very soon to know each other; we talked freely, you were very kind, and I of course liked you for that. Next I learned to esteem you, for I thought you just and good. I fancied a native love of right, interwoven with every lineament of your noble features, and expressed in every air of your manly bearing. In short, from our little acquaintance, I have gathered the impression that you are a generous, high-souled nature, tnat you had rather lay down your life than condescend to a wrong act. I prize your friendship, and evermore, if it be your pleasure, I will count you in the list of my corresponding friends. Let the world frown ever so darkly, or prosperity smile ever so charmingly, it will be all the same; in my confidence and simple affections there will ever be a place for you; and as you said in your good-by to Mrs. H——, "once in a very long time think just a little of me," so I will say to you. Think of me only when you can get no subject of thought more engaging, or find feelings to share more congenial. Could you have looked back on us the day after you left, and beheld what a gap your departure made in our circle, I think you would have acknowledged yourself complimented, if not a little flattered. Every time the ladies met they regretted your departure, but the gentlemen sat round in the piazza grinning, as if they were glad of it. That little Swede has so stepped into the good graces of the young ladies, that they have nearly adopted him Beau General, in your place. He has told me many little incidents of his history which interest me much. Since he has been in our country, he has supported his aged father by his hard earnings, the poor man meantime supposing his son amassing a fortune in the New World. He knew the Bremers, and his accounts of them are very pleasing.

Dr. R——— plays matron this week, and the patients do nothing but brag of their fare, and say no more about going away. We have such excellent bread and delicious griddle-cakes; and such *magnificent* mush, so coarse ground, the kernels must have been cracked three into one. You write very enticingly of the City, but you have no sea breeze there, no hills to gaze upon, no Sound, no beautiful bay and woods with sleeping lakes among; no brooks where to wander, or hills to climb.

I received a note from my good friend Mr. D ——, to-day, from which I infer he has not received mine by you. Please get it to him as soon as convenient. Kind regards to your fun-making brother. May he always be merry as now—oh no, I will take that back. Reverses and disappointments make us considerate. We are here to be prepared for another life, and the course best for us our Heavenly Father will mark out, and thither our footsteps must fall. Be wise, be good, be truthful to thyself, and fear God, that thou mayest be happy here, and numbered with the blest hereafter.

P. S. The long road you taught us over the hill, Kate and I walk three times every day; often stopping on the brow of it, to roll the stones far below. Then we trudge on, talking sometimes delightedly and sometimes sadly. Do not indulge too freely in those good things, or you will have to return here, where you know self-denial is not only a virtue but part of the treatment.

Yesterday a party of us sailed up the Sound, and passed an hour in the house where General Washington, soon after the war, in his tour of Long Island, stopped over night with his friend Daniel Young. A son of the same gentleman resides there still, but his head is covered with the "garniture of the grave," and like the roof that shelters him, he must soon fall to the earth.

Long Island Water Cure, Aug. 1848.

My Good Friend Mr. D.:—I have waited these many days hoping to find a hand long enough *above* water to write you. The sail in company with your excellent friend, Vice Chancellor McC. and Mrs. N., (to whom he introduced me soon after you left,) was delightful indeed. The briny air of the Sound was free and bracing, and over *those peaches* our chat was more like the meeting of familiar friends, than the growing converse of strangers.

Dr. S. met me at the landing, as you and he had arranged, and his cordial reception quite banished all my fears. It was the same at the house; indeed they all seemed to know me, and as they gathered round, one after another, for introductions, I verily thought myself breathing a new atmosphere, and shaking hands with the people from a climate at least forty degrees warmer than Institution latitude. Pardon my detail, but I wish to tell you as much as possible of the kindness of Dr. S. He seated me at table next himself, directly opposite Mrs. N., and every attention possible has so far been paid me.

We have a very pleasant company of ladies. The gentlemen are representatives of almost every nation, all however very affable and entertaining. An English officer, who was wounded while engaged in the Queen's service in India, seems a sort of walking Encyclopedia, a perfect embodiment of general intelligence; this, united with an eloquent voice, makes him quite the intellectual star of our circle, and as we are allowed no time for reading, it is fortunate to have such an inexhaustible fund to draw from. There is a gentleman here too from St. Petersburgh, whose father was a Russian general, his mother a Polish lady, and when the country of the latter struck for freedom, the son "bared his breast" for the land of his mother, and of course can return to his home no more. He is gallant as a knight, and affable as a Frenchman, and more kind and attentive to the wants of all, than any one here.

Knowing this to be the resort of invalids, I expected to find all very quiet and sad, but a more merry group I never met. Here, to get well, the patients have a round of duties to perform, each tasked according to his ability. Indeed exercise is an important part of the treatment. When I arrived, some were playing ball, others were returning from long walks; some singing, playing the piano, organ, guitar, violin, and so on. We have one subject of conversation which never wears out, that is, *diet*, *diet*. They say it is the same at all establishments of this kind; the treatment makes people hungry; and besides, we are obliged to live plainly, and one meal is no sooner over, than little groups in the piazza and all around are talking about what they will have to eat the next time. Some have their food weighed to them. Eight ounces of coarse bread, or its equivalent, is, I believe, all that many are allowed.

Dr. S. is at present giving us a course of lectures upon Shrotes' theory of the Hunger Cure. This is indeed the strangest thing I have heard yet, starving a man to make him well. Shrotes' establishment is a little way up the mountain beyond Priessnitz. Dr. S. says he actually saw and conversed with a man there, who had not tasted food nor water for seven days, save what his body drank in from the surface, as he was every day several hours rolled in damp sheets.

Dr. N., President of Union College, is here, receiving treatment for inflammatory rheumatism. When he came he was moved only in his arm-chair, which has a wheel on each side, and so constructed that he rolls it himself by means of two levers. This morning he walked a little way on the piazza alone, and oh ! how delighted he was, but he is yet a very great sufferer. A friend in New-York sends him every morning a basket of choice fruit, from which I am often favored. Mrs. N. has promised me a ride in their little three-wheeled carriage, a kind of vehicle that I never saw.

My health is certainly improving; cold water or something else has so shocked my nervous energies into life, that I can already walk several miles in a day. The treatment is not so disagreeable as I feared, and on the whole I am passing my time very pleasantly. Indeed I am entering into the full spirit of the water cure, and its every variety of bath. However, Mr. D., I shall heed your caution to examine every day my fingers and toes, and when I see them showing any signs of being connected by those thin membraneous substances, known to naturalists as *webs*, I will most assuredly, as you say, ask the doctor for his bill, and hurry home; for I have no idea of joining any of the finny tribes, whatever else may become of me. I can hardly think it possible that you wrote your last in an atmosphere heated to 92° Fahrenheit. Indeed if Hamlet had been with you, he might have realized personally his prayer—

"Oh that this too, too solid flesh would melt,
Thaw, and resolve itself into a dew."

You say, if Hydropathy, Allopathy and Homœpathy fail, there is still left Chrono-Thermal treatment. I do not know what that is, but fancy I should prefer Shrotes' fasting plan as my "*dernier resort.*"

New-York Institution for the Blind,
March 22nd, 1849.

When I heard of the cholera in New Orleans, I easily imagined the sad dilemma you were in. I saw you in the lonely hotel treading the floor, then stopping short, lost in troubled thought. I saw too the shadow of gloom that settled on your brow, and though far away, be assured I shared your fears, for I knew it was not for yourself you were suffering. Is it not possible that we have misnamed a part of our Heavenly Father's dispensations, for coming as they do, all from the same hand, why are they not all good? I wish I could say something this morning that would divest you of every care, and banish every shade from your thoughts. But the bravest and best have been those whose pilgrim feet were oftenest torn. * * * * *

Across the way are some Germans, among them a young Baron who is sorely distressed, and my heart aches for him. Though but nineteen years old he has passed the ordeal of the Mexican war, and is now suffering its painful consequences. God pity the youth whose inexperienced feet have wandered so far from his home, where he has no one to speak an encouraging word or lead him again in the right way. His brother is one of the principal actors in the present revolutions of Germany, and his poor mother writes that her pillow is never dry from her tears for her lost son.

When Julian was here last we went to see him. What a good creature Julian is; he seems to me the very personation of truthfulness and benevolence. I wish you could have heard his encouraging advice to that young Baron. Beside being unsophisticated and unassuming, he is nobly generous, frank, and straightforward as a sunbeam; united with the artless innocence of youth, he possesses the stirring energies of a man, and that uncompromising integrity which characterizes all his ways, must secure him success in any undertaking. He seems very much pleased with that little Miss A., but says he is not in a position to marry, so you see he is discreet withal.

Sometimes he brings up his guitar, and really he plays and sings with a great deal of taste.

* * * * * * * * *

Well, it has at last come to this: they say I must get *my home* by making a book, and advise me to publish a little volume of my letters. Mr. C. and Mr. D. say they will help me all they can, and I am half a mind to undertake it. Do not say one discouraging word, for I have already too many fears to insure success. But never mind; I shall yet by some means have that little cottage, little parlor, little kitchen, and little cook, little carriage, little pony, little driver, and all that sort of thing. My amanuensis is laughing,—I suppose she is thinking what gay times you will all have when you come to see me, and Mr. M. too, with his wife and fortune. Mr. B. better hurry up, for Mr. M. does not bring so many *oranges* here for nothing ; besides, you know S. is very susceptible of the tender emotion. I hope neither of them will trifle with her feelings, for with her such an injury would be irreparable, as she is so inexperienced in such matters.

I have just two things more to write you : first, I anticipate your visit to New-York, second, I hope it will be soon, and for the sake of euphony I will add a third ; there is no good in this life that I do not pray may be yours. I have always told you more prosperous days will come ; and I feel now that their dawning has begun. Put on your feet the sandals of sincerity, fastened with the buckles of integrity; bind about your heart the noble principles of Christianity ; in a word, take up yourself just as you are, and go forth. If barriers are in the way, wait not to remove them, but, like the heroes of old, boldly tread them down ; and when the sun has crossed the sky a few more times, you will be in possession of what you so much desire.

You say my friend Sarah is beautiful ; more

than that, she is good. I have never known a young lady across whose mind the shadow of change so seldom falls. As you see her first, so she is ever after, joyous, kind and affectionate; Mrs. S., her aunt, is a very model of female excellence; and her son Willie is well worthy such a mother. But the rest of them are mortals like myself.

You and David must visit fast as possible. Try on each other's coats and hats, and exclaim, "What perfect fits!" pay each other compliments, as you gentlemen do, get angry, make up friends, &c. &c., then set your face eastward. I give you leave to stop in R., and say all the nice things possible to Miss M., only so you say them fast. But you and Sibyl need not flatter yourselves that I shall again sit quiet and let you two talk all the time; and spar, and cast out your leads to sound each other; not a bit of it. I knew you long first, and old claims should always be regarded; besides you are not to look at her while you talk to me either. I will leave it to David if I am not right, and not at all exacting.

I wish there was in this world one other spirit that now and then could fly off in tangent raptures, like poor Ned. Why, they might have all the ecstasies of seven worlds crowded into this one little terraqueous wheeling orb, and yet talk of brighter days to come. He has come home again from the South, with his head so completely turned with admiration for *that* little Creole, that he talks of her all the time, when not abusing his bad English.

Geneva, June, 1848.

Cousin Will:—I have lived long enough to learn that things are not always what they seem. As ripples play lightly upon the smooth surface of a summer sea, while far below dark and turbid waters are waiting the storm-god to move them to fury, so a smiling brow, often conceals a storm of revengeful passion. Words of love and friendship often tremble on the lips, while curses nestle in the heart. So all through life, things are not what they seem.

A show of affluence is often as true an index of poverty, as want itself. The poorest of the metals is often mistaken for the richest coin; so by means of art and worldly tact, man may palm off his ignorance for knowledge, and his vice for virtue. So again, a man of wisdom, clad in mean attire, and surrounded by homely circumstances, may be as easily mistaken for the ignorant and unaspiring. When the motive is not known or appreciated, how differently the act appears; and we find ourselves to-day censuring a deed which to-morrow we may loudly applaud. Therefore, "Be not wise in thine own conceit," and "Judge not, that ye be not judged," are sayings worthy of all acceptation. The youth who to-day plays on the green with a herd of other ragged lads, observed but to be pitied, may in a few years contend honors with La Place and Newton, and read titles with Lord Rosse and the starry Le Verrier.

* * * * *

My dear Mrs. Snow.—I have no "sight-seeings in Europe" to picture you, no history of blood and tears to write, no storms of ocean, nor clustered beauties of Naples, and its rival bay Rio Janeiro to describe, nor *ruins* to paint, save those of a broken heart; among which the voice of buried love ever moans, like the sighings of decay amid fallen temples and mouldering castles.

We have our preferences as well for things as persons. Of all the trees on these grounds I love most this branching mulberry; it shades me oftenest when the sun is bright, and when the night dews are heavy on its leaves, it covers still my brow, till long after the moon has waned and many stars have set. Oh, never breathe to human ear thy sorrow, but soothe thy grief in humble prayer; and when thy full heart goes up to Heaven, let none but spirits hear.

My hand has become a perfect truant, placing the letters now on one side of the line, and now on the other; to remedy this we use a grooved card under the paper and write with a pencil, which accounts for the strange-looking sheet I send you. Not long since I heard Dr. T—— say in a sermon, "it is a principle of our nature to prize that highest we are most troubled to get;" no matter, then, if you are puzzled a little to decipher these erratic words.

Four weeks ago our school closed; and a party of some fifty went on board the Santa Claus for Albany, thence by the cars to their respective residences. Others on the same day left for *their* homes in New-York and its vicinity, till very, very few were left. Night came, and the halls and corridors, so accustomed to echo with merry laugh and tread, and sounds of music, from the large organ down to the trumpet whistle, were all silent; and *departure* seemed whispered every where. Little Henry, who ran back to the sick room once more to say *good-by* to poor Jakey, was unfortunately left. When he returned to the lower hall, behold, the omnibuses were far away, and nothing could call them back or stay their progress. We tried to comfort him, but all his full heart *could* say was, "*I want to go home.*"

The moon was on the hills, the stars came out, and the shades of night had fallen beautifully on all the weary world; we were sleeping forgetful and happy, when suddenly the spacious dormitory, the chapel, and all the empty rooms were filled with sweet sounds, which seemed pouring in at the windows and sifting down from among the trees. "What is it, and where is it?" every one starting up, almost wondering if the spirits of the Blind had not come back to serenade those they had left. "The Bird Waltz," says one, as its chirpings were echoing every where; it was none other than the Christies themselves, gathered among the firs in the front yard to give our loneliness a serenade. They played long and beautifully. Lovely May and other of their Ethiopian songs were never half so sweet, for which we could make them no compliments. We had no bouquets to toss them, no lamps to light, and could only enjoy their music in silence; but when our quick ears followed their departing footsteps, our love and gratitude would have turned their harps to gold, such as minstrels wake beyond the sky.

In the morning, as each seemed to know better the feelings of the other, we were more silent, and our breakfast had little relish. One after another left the dining-room, till, when the moment came for the bell, there were none to dismiss. I took my portfolio and came to this favorite tree. Presently the girls began to pass, walking as usual, two and two, with their arms encircling each other's waist, for the mutual protection it affords. Says one to her mate, "During vacation I will teach you six songs, with the symphonies and accompaniments, if you will teach me those Herz's Exercises you know, and some pieces of Mozart and Haydn." "Agreed," was the reply; "I will tell you one of them now, and then we will go and practise it." Said another, "When I finish my spread, I'm going to knit a purse and bag to send to my aunt." Another, "I shall knit nothing but star and oak-leaf tidies this vacation, and one coat for a present to little Georgie;" so they went on, "innocent creatures," crossing again and again the angling walks, some counting the positions and bars of music, some planning pastimes, and others wondering who of their mates had reached *Home*.

"Come, sit you down here, girls," said I, "and I will tell you a story, if you please." "Oh! good, good," exclaimed every one, and in a moment they were all planted upon the green sward, in the best listening mood possible. I told them the tale of "Aunt Mercy," after which we arranged to meet every morning, and I was to repeat, as well as memory could bring it back, a chapter of Warren's "Now and Then," which Mr. Hastings read to me last winter. Then each in her turn promised to do the same from some volume which *she* had heard. Little Jenny begged to be excused, said she never *could* keep awake the reading hour, and had forgotten all the stories she ever heard. Caty complained that it always took all her time to keep Helen still, so she had heard none of the reading matter either. Unless she could think of something better, Mary proposed treating us to some of

Wilson's "Tales of the Border." Maggie spoke of some chapters from the "Diary of a Physician," but, said she, they *all* end *so* sadly.

Employment is truly the chariot-wheel of the soul; without it we only drag weary existence along. The morning wore away, and the two months' vacation began to seem a little life-time, and all the days "*dark* and *dreary.*"

Towards evening, to my delight and astonishment, Miss S. returned. "Get your bonnet and shawl," said she. "I could not go to Boston, and leave you here so lonely; I have come to take you to Brooklyn, to stop a little time with some friends;" and the last two weeks I passed at the delightful home of Mr. and Mrs. Emory, and Mr. Augustus Graham, a very interesting old gentlemen, if indeed it is at all proper to call a man *old*, merely because the frosts of many winters have blanched his locks and deepened the furrows on his brow, while he still retains the mental freshness of youth and all the acting excellence of half his years. Mr. Graham is a native of Edinburgh, educated in London; some fifty years since he came to New-York, where by his own industry and economy he has amassed a fortune which now, in his declining years, he is distributing for the relief of the unfortunate and distressed, with a hand as liberal and free as the heart of benevolence and philanthropy could ask.

On our Nation's last birth-day, Mr. Graham presented to the Brooklyn Institute and Hospital the pretty sum of fifty thousand. Oh, who would not wish the power of dispensing good so freely? In a word, who would not like to be rich? Mr. Graham's apartments are caskets of choice books, paintings, engravings, &c. One day, speaking of Paris, he placed in my hands a little relic of the Bastile, which he procured as follows: Passing over the grounds, and finding nothing worth preserving, the guide took him around by the outer wall, where he spied, far up in a niche, a figure bereft of every limb that seemed *breakable*, save one finger, pointing in lone astonishment to the shades of misery which must ever haunt the grounds of the Bastile. Being a pretty good Benjamite, Mr. G. threw a stone and felled the finger to the ground. "Come," said the guide, "we had best be going from this place, or those guards will be after us." So Mr. G. pocketed quickly his well-earned relic, and walked away. The finger has on it the indenture of the nail and the little creases of the first and second joint, as perfectly as though chiselled but now.

Institution for the Blind.

My good friend Mr. D.:—When I look over the past I cannot see that either in my letters or interviews I have ever added to your mind one pleasing thought, and yet you bear with me.

The veneration I ever feel for your worth and character so silence my words and restrain my actions, when in your presence, that I often think that you may with good reason suppose me wanting in the grateful love I should cherish for so valuable a friend. But believe me, Mr. D., if your dear Augusta and Juliet were my own sisters, I could not love and esteem you more.

My remaining sight you probably value as little as I do ; but *this* I do desire, to see the time when my eyes will cease to trouble me. I cannot arrange sentences sufficient for a letter, listen to an hour's reading, or practise the least, or spend an evening in conversation, but the morbid irritation in the nerves and muscles of my eyes becomes so painful as to keep me awake nearly the whole night. Three years I have submitted passively to the prescriptions and decisions of the faculty, never once lifting my voice approvingly or otherwise.

Last summer the advice of all the doctors was, " Go to the springs ; showering and bathing will do more for you than medicine." But that was impossible. Others again urged me to return and try the water-cure in New-York. To that various objections were raised ; indeed I knew nothing of it myself until a friend gave it a very satisfactory trial. She has a miniature apparatus, douche and shower-bath in her own house, which I used some time last winter with much benefit both to my general health and eyes. Now, you see Mr. D. what I am at : I do very much wish to pass one week or two in the water-cure establishment somewhere in New-York. I have a conviction that it will both remedy my dyspepsia and consequent irritation of my eyes. May I make the experiment?

My spirit sees no look of disapproval in your thoughts. However, you will tell me plainly what you think of it, and your words shall be my *oracle;* I will ask no other. Pray pardon me for troubling you, and believe that I only desire to know and do the right.

Stone Cottage, June, 1849.

* * * * * * * * *

An hour ago I bathed in the crystal waters that flow fast by the cottage door, then with Mary followed up their winding way, treading on the soft shadows of nightfall, which come to sleep among the bushes and flowers.

This afternoon we crossed the bridge up the hill road to the wood, and deep in its shade sat us down, and opened the book which Mary had brought to read. So every day, with my head pillowed in her lap, and her little hand on my brow, I beguile the hours which otherwise were long and weary.

The clouds are thick about me, I cannot see the face of one Angel, nor hear the flitting of a wing, nor the echo of a harp, nor one whisper on the breeze. My heart is hard and I cannot weep. I am not good or I were more blessed and more happy, and more like the sweet spirits, who with folded pinions linger unseen above our pathway, ever beckoning us on in the good and right way.

Oh that I could dissolve my thoughts and mould them anew, free from all evil. Oh, that in the light of heaven I could whiten my immortal nature from all the stains which sin has made. Then my soul would put on her wings and go to breathe the expansive airs of heaven, and seize upon the revelations of her spiritual being, and learn her destiny in the future life, whither to our shortsightedness the way is unmarked, and to our weak faith and little courage her realities are solemn and fearful, and when we would enter there and grow familiar with its white scenes, something earthly draws us back, and whispers, "not yet, no, not yet." Oh, my soul, when wilt thou be ready? when will thy work be done? when wilt thou rise and set thy house in order, and see to it that thy charities be all numbered, and thy goods be distributed to the poor, and hasten thy feet to the abodes of the distressed, set thy hand to smooth the pillow of the sick, and place cooling waters to his fevered lips? Thy field of labor is in this life, and what thou wouldst do for God, thou must do for his creatures

---

Institution for the Blind, June 12th, 1848.

FRIEND MUMFORD:—I find here so little incident, so little that is sufficiently suggestive to awaken and call forth those lively emotions which make the soul of epistolary writing, that I really approach it with diffidence.

Besides, you must not expect me to invest my pages with that coloring and vivacity that

I would, were I mingling more with the world. Retirement is favorable to sentiment, but pent-up feelings die, and unexpressed and unshared thoughts do wither.

We are so constituted that suggestive society of some kind is needful, as well for our health and happiness as our mental culture. Thinking is perhaps a more healthful exercise for the mind than reading, for books are but the symbols of thought and feeling; and as the substance is preferred to the shadow, so the original is better than the copy. The sources of conversation and locality from which we can derive any positive improvement, cover only a little space in the learned world; to the active mind, hardly more than the boundary that girts the infant's cradle.

The future is unknown. We have not an eye like the Infinite, to pierce its dark veil, and read its mystic lore. To the past, then, we must go for knowledge, and books are its only chronicles, the only caskets in which its priceless pearls are set. To me the temples of knowledge are all barred, and its fountains are dried or turned to rocks, and I have no power to bring again their gushing waters. I may no more drink from the streams of Pieria, or sip the dews of Castalia.

Evermore mine is the brow of night, whose stars are set. Flowers are at my feet, and dews like diamonds are scattered all around, but the light is gone, and I cannot see them. Grief has long had a place in my heart, and melancholy and sorrow have been familiar; but to-day something like the shadow of despair is nestling there. Oh God! save me, save me, oh God! There is a wildness in my thoughts, a dread, a torturing fear that is swallowing up my very life in wretchedness, more than words can speak. How real sorrow doth deceive the world! She weeps the long night away, and at morn puts on a sunny brow to meet those around her; and while they wonder at her cheerful joy, she answers well and wisely too; "ills are only severe blessings, and when received with a prepared heart, they do us the greater good." Besides, if we would please others, we must ourselves at least *seem* to be pleased; and it is well when, as Goldsmith says of the French, we grow to be what we seem. Common pity mixed with common scorn I do despise, my soul loathes the very word; but give me your friendship growing from esteem, and I will thank you and love you too; and such as my poor heart has will I give in return, and perhaps in our little commerce we may both grow richer.

You remember deaf Maggie. To-day I engaged to entertain her, but her senseless gibberings have wearied and sickened every feeling, till my spirit cries, "How long, Oh Lord! how long?" One can play the philanthropist to the low and ignorant, and share their little thoughts, and if possible try to lift them higher, and with ready delight minister to their wants; but to be ever companioned with them, to be herded one of them, is hard to bear.

My whole nature thirsts for a higher and more improving intercourse, and longs to feast again upon the beauties of kindling and inspiring thoughts. We are progressive beings, and our every act, every thought or emotion, should be a step in our *progressive life.* As the least blow upon this little earth, in its acting and reacting force is felt through the illimitable fields of space, and that eternally, so man's most simple word or feeling, in its effects will remain unmeasured, when matter's last atom shal. have wandered back to that chaos, whence it came forth.

You say you make no claims to genius; very true; but you have what in my opinion should be prized far more, an entire set of strong natural powers, developed by early culture, disciplined by self-application, and inspired by the love of truth. Such a mind may begin where genius leaves off, and I see no reason why you may not cope with Newton in his measurement of the spheres, or follow the heaven-led operations of Milton's mind; ascend the intellectual throne of Bacon, or handle the more weighty reasonings of Locke.

The pathway that meanders up the steeps of Parnassus is laid open, and he who kindles his aspirations with ambition's fire may scale its dizzy heights, where, with the key of science in his hand, he may unlock the mysteries of nature; decipher the symbols that hide the Chald's sublimer lore; may read the finger-marks of Him whose hand has spread the starry cope, and strown with gems the ocean cave. Nature, in converse with him, will speak in her own familiar tongue. With the finger of philosophy he may grasp the "lightning's fiery wing," may rend asunder the air, impearl the briny wave, that since time's dawn has lashed the beachen shore. The decomposition of the granite rock of the everlasting hills shall be to him but the amusement of an hour. With La Place, he may feel all the tremblings of the waning moon; with Plato's ravished ears he may list the music of the chanting spheres, till his spirit plumes its pinions, and, with flight sublime, soars to Truth's occult abode. * * *

P. S. I forgot to tell you that it is vacation, and in the absence of Miss M., Sibyl is playing matron in the most dignified and judicious manner; that is, the casks in the store-room are being freely relieved of their deposits, as, you know, she believes in a circulating medium tending to the *general good.*

Long Island Water-Cure, Sept. 12, 1848.

MY GOOD FRIEND MR. D.:—Your note came yesterday, and the parcel last evening. Mrs. Nott has returned. She read your letter, then gave me an account of her very pleasant interview. It is certainly gratifying to have persons so knowing and so good as Mr. D. and Mrs. N., so kindly interested in my poor behalf. But oh, how gladly would I relieve all my friends of farther anxiety. Yes, how gladly would I put forth my hand to meet my own wants. Sometimes this feeling does so possess me, that I am almost desirous of relieving the world of one so troublesome, but never more shall I be sufficient to myself. I am in the world, and cannot conveniently get out of it. So I am in the hands of God. He has placed me among my fellows, and veiled my eyes, perhaps as much to try them as me, for certainly, go where I will, I am always tasking some *hand*, and sharing the generous sympathies of some heart.

I am certainly much more strong and

healthful than when I came here. The nerves of my eyes are still very weak and irritable, though their inflamed appearance is rapidly leaving them. Dr. —— asked me the other day how I would like to pass the winter here; I replied, "I should be most happy to do so, but that is quite impossible." He then asked if I could be as contented here as at the Institution; I told him "this was a world of delight compared with it, setting aside all considerations of health." He then remarked, "I think we must keep you here through the winter, we shall be less in number then, and more like a family." Now what idea the Dr. had of my staying here, is more than I can conceive; it does not seem possible that he thinks of extending his kindness so far, to one whom he knows so little. And surely he has no reason to expect a compensation, from any source which I can imagine; so, in all probability I shall leave here two weeks from Wednesday.

I have gathered many ideas of correct living which I value exceedingly; besides, I have made very many pleasing acquaintances, of whom I will tell you more by and by.

If my poor eyes were well, I would write a course of letters from here, and the many things I could say of Dr. ——'s establishment, might do a little to compensate him for the great kindness he has shown me. Not that I could add any thing to the much that has been said, but you know sometimes the simple, unvarnished story of a patient, tells more in favor of the doctor than all of his long and well-written essays upon Materia Medica, Theory and Practice.

Indeed when I come home, I shall do little but preach cold water, and plain diet; for certainly Hydropathy has not a more thorough convert. All the ladies read your letter, and laughed much at *that slip of your pen.*

Mrs. Judge N——, of Ohio, is a patient here; she was delighted with your remarks on woman, and said they accorded precisely with her husband's views.

Then Mrs. B—— is really getting well! Thank God for so great a favor. We could not spare her. The world is very dark and lonely now, notwithstanding I have so many friends, so many loved ones. I have this morning unfortunately glanced a little beyond the coming two weeks, and consequently a shade of sadness covers my thoughts; but no matter, all will be well.

Kind regards to your dear family. Mr. Briggs is probably again with you: you are indeed among the favored. I think of your Sabbaths all day. Do not forget, I am to hear Mr. ———'s Thanksgiving sermon, and the first after his return from Europe.

Now, good-by, Mr. D———, with as much gratitude and love as my simple heart can hold.

P. S. I do not much regret the delay of my note, since it came to you so illustriously companioned. How the simple thing must have blushed being read, while your thoughts were full of words from the burning pen of the Sage of Ashland.

Stone Cottage, August, 1849.

COUSIN WILL :—Your last poem pleases me exceedingly. I see you have truly the soul of a poet, and I very well understand your desire to travel, and apparent dissatisfaction with the tame way in which you are passing your time. No one more than I would like you to see the wind-god shake old ocean by his mane, and feast your eye on the Alps and Apennines, and watch their lakes when "red morn glows on their breasts." But, Cousin Will, a poet too well fed, or too much indulged, is apt to lose his muse. It is *hard* blows you need instead of gentle ones. You are an only child, the pride of doting parents, and your home is lined with books and papers, and you have tutors and masters always at hand. Hence if I sympathize at all with you, it will be because you are too much favored; for if we lift the curtain of the past, and backward wander, however far, we find written in legible characters upon every page of man's history—no excellence is obtained without labor. Poverty, Cousin Will, is the nursery of genius, and toil he must who would excel in any course, or have it said of him, he was great or good. Young men of affluence, having little else to do than feast upon the bounties which Providence has assigned them, and bask in the dawn of new enjoyments, are but seldom disposed to contend for meeds of honor, obtained only at the expense of unwearied application and self-denial.

But they often enter the literary course, and for a time may walk in advance of those less favored than themselves, until by self-indulgence and irresolution, they become effeminate; fluctuate, and, to their mortification, yield the palm to their poor but persevering competitors; who gradually advance step by step, treading down every obstruction, and boldly surmounting every barrier; nor tarrying in all the mountain way until they reach the goal, and grasp the object of their anxious but deferred hopes.

The orb of science never shone so brightly on Egypt's monuments of art and grandeur, as when her poor youth, whose eyes beamed with native intelligence, were sought after, and welcomed to her classic halls and bowers. And the Grecian stage was favored with its richest productions, while those priests of nature who dwelt in the upland caves, came down bare-headed and bare-footed, to be the worthy competitors of kings.

In Rome, the seven-hilled city of Fame, whose halls are stored with the treasures of intellect, we find the richest gems of which the world can boast. But the fathers of her philosophy and poetry had no other claims to distinction or honor, than those of true merit. And could we map to our view the panorama of six thousand years, we would, in every age and in every land, find those to whom science owes her improvements, those who have worshipped at the shrine of art, those whose hands have guided safely the helm in the hour of a nation's peril, were not only deprived of the luxuries of life, but were often strangers to its most common comforts. And while toiling in their onward and upward way, the aristocracy of wealth frowned upon them; and while they battled bravely life's pitiless storms, persecuting slander often hurled her envenomed arrows at their venerable and defenceless heads; and but for that unyielding and obstinate determination which never fails, they had, with the multitude, passed unknown away.

We see the high-minded philosopher, Galileo, soliciting the loan of a few shillings to purchase materials for constructing an instrument with which he afterwards shook the great foundations of error. Tycho Brahe said, if he owed the world any thing, it was for its untiring opposition. The learned Kepler said his life had been only a scene of wants and privations. Rollin, a star of moral beauty, ran when a boy with the herd of other ragged lads to say mass; but that ethereal spirit, which beamed from his eagle eye and expansive brow, snatched him a gem from the mud, and bade him shine for ever in the splendors of his own genius.

Columbus, whose soul when unfurled "leaped across the sea and laid bare a world," you know, lived and died stung to his heart's core with want and neglect. The richest minds England has produced were pearls brought up from the darkest obscurity. Kirke White, the genius of musings; Shakspeare, tc whom nature gave her magic wand; Chatterton, Sir Humphrey Davy, and his student the bookbinder, in a coarse frock, now no less than Chemist Royal.

Napoleon, when he saw his ranks becoming thin, grasped the standard in his own hand, rushed forward, leaping over bodies of the slain like a spirit of the storm till the victory was his. Thus have arisen to excellence multitudes with whom the Fates loved to war. So there are moments in the lives of all when a word, a resolve, or a single step seems to be a pivot upon which their whole destiny turns either for weal or woe ; and that moment with you, Cousin Will, is now. During the late war a British battery, stationed upon a hill, considerably annoyed our troops ; "Can you storm that battery?" said General Ripley to Colonel Miller. "I will try, Sir," was the laconic answer. Now, only rise and arm your most lofty aspirations with Colonel Miller's weapon, and victory is yours. The world is the great drama upon which each individual is to act his part with honor or infamy, as he will himself choose; but there is a fame which will last when the skies of worldly glory are darkened, and her scrolls have gone to decay; upon her pure escutcheon are written the "names of those whom the love of God has blest;" whose hands have helped to plant the great standard of reform and the amelioration of mankind; who have added their vial to the river whose waters flow for the healing of the nations. Continue in the paths of virtue, daily adding to your stores of knowledge from those valuable receptacles of the wisdom of all ages—books. Seek to shine like some of the jewels which decorate the temple of our freedom, and leave your name with those to whose memory rock-hewn monuments are but mockery. Try to be great in the spirit of God, like John Wesley, John Newton, and our Edwards, the vein of whose eloquence flowed only to fertilize the desolation of the human heart.

The most powerful imagination, is that which embodies truth in living characters; and the most imperishable fame is the memory of him who made the world better by living in it.

Union College, Schenectady, June 26th, 1849.

MY GOOD FRIEND MR. D.:—You are such a devotee to science and literature, or, in other words, such a devourer of books, and every thing in the way of intelligence, it seems fitting I should write to you while at one of the finest seats of learning in our State, and at the feet of one greater than Gamaliel.

Dr. Nott, you are aware, has been forty-five years President of this Institution. He passed, yesterday, his seventy-sixth birth-day, apparently in possession of as many physical and mental energies as are ordinarily the companions of men of half his years—hearing his classes, attending to all the calls of his students, listening to and correcting their rhetorical exercises, preparatory to the coming commencement.

In the morning, while the Doctor was reading the papers, a committee of the senior class waited upon him, requesting permission to have a general college celebration of his birthday. At this the good sage seemed much surprised, and asked, "How in the world did you learn that? Really, I did not know it myself; but if it be so, boys, that I am another year older, and you wish to celebrate it, you must do it in the way I am going to—work with all your might." "But," said they, "we would like to illuminate the college." "Illuminate the college!" said he, "why what an idea! such a thing was never done." "Why yes," said the students, "the first year you came here it was illuminated." "Not hardly," said the doctor, "for if I remember rightly, we had no college to illuminate." "But," said they, "they hung the lamps in the trees, which meant the same thing." So the dialogue went on, and at last terminated by the Doctor's consenting to let the senior class come to his house in the evening, for an informal levee, specifying that they should all go home precisely at ten o'clock.

The older I grow, the more I see how averse the learned and sensible always are to any thing like show or ostentation. During the day many old and tried friends called upon the Doctor and his lady, and offered their congratulations that another year had been added to his long and useful life; hoping that he would be spared to them many more. Many presents were sent in, among them a beautiful bouquet to Mrs. Nott, and to the Doctor a large ripe orange of domestic growth, with stem and leaves still attached. Mc——, who you know is figuring so largely as a statesman, sent by express an engraving of himself, large as life, and elegantly framed, accompanied by a note. While Mrs. Nott and Professor Potter were selecting the most appropriate place for hanging it, the Doctor says, "I have it, hang him in the college library, where he should have been himself long ago. But a fine fellow that Mc——, and he knows a pretty good deal too, notwithstanding."

The professors and their ladies, the tutors and other officers of the college, were present at the party, and altogether the evening passed both profitably and pleasantly. The Doctor was in fine spirits, entertaining the groups who thronged about him, with vivid delineations of the master-spirits of the last generation, with most of whom he was intimate. Some one asked him whether he thought Hamilton or Webster the greater man? He replied, Hamilton, for Webster has lived to do much since Hamilton died; and besides, the greatest efforts of Hamilton have never been published.

Through his long life, the Doctor has been a devoted student of eloquence; this is as evident in his common conversation, as from his sermons and writings. His words are not so select, as his manner is impressive; consequently you cannot hear him speak, without being more or less influenced. The best feature in the evening's entertainment was the good Doctor's address to the whole assembly. He dwelt with great emphasis upon the fact, that men do not live out half their days, in consequence of infractions upon the physical laws of their being. He said one-fifth of the human race die before they are twelve months old, one-third before they are two years, and one-half before they are twenty. Now nothing analogous to this is found among other animals; all other species live, with but few exceptions, to a certain and uniform age. Whence, then, this fearful mortality among men? If you give as a reason the fall of Adam, to this I reply, that even after the fall of Adam men lived to near a thousand years. The truth is, young gentlemen, that man, the only animal endowed with reason and the higher attributes, is almost the only animal that outrages the plain and obvious laws of his nature. The Doctor then, by way of illustration, remarked upon his own plain mode of living, his constant use of cold baths, and his abstaining from all stimulants, both in food and drink. Life, said he, is the most precious of Heaven's gifts, and I have no doubt all before me would like to extend it to the greatest numbei of years possible. In the early part of the evening, one of the students, Mr. McCoy, (a young man of decided talent,) read aloud some very appropriate passages from the bard of Avon, one from Henry IV., another from the speech of Adam in "As you like it;" which seemed written almost expressly for the occasion and the venerable person for whom it was selected:

> "Though I look old, yet I am strong and lusty:
> For in my youth I never did apply
> Hot and rebellious liquors in my blood,
> Nor did not with unbashful forehead woo
> The means of weakness and debility;
> Therefore my age is as a lusty winter,
> Frosty, but kindly."

Just before the company dispersed, the venerable Doctor referred in a touching manner to the separation that would soon take place between the teachers and the class before him, and besought them to live in constant reference to the judgment-day, to prepare for which all others are given. "I charge you," said he, "let not one before me, on that tremendous day, be absent from the right hand of God; that should it be my happiness to be found there also, I may be permitted to exclaim, '*Here, Lord, am I, and the children Thou hast committed to my care.*'" And then in behalf of all present, offered a most affecting and solemn prayer to the Father of all our mercies. His reference to the pestilence that walketh in darkness, and the destruction that wasteth at noonday, was very affecting. In compliance with his petition, one could almost see the destroying angel returning his raging sword to the scabbard, and pronouncing it enough.

This morning we had a delightful drive in the Doctor's three-wheeled buggy which is a singular sort of vehicle, but exceedingly convenient for getting in and out, besides it is quite impossible to upset it.

I enjoy Mrs. Nott's society here even more than at Long Island, she is so amiable and lovely. Though there is seemingly no end to her duties and calls, yet she always finds a little time tor every one. The most important star in all the sky shines with a mild but steady ray; such is ever the influence and power of woman; noiseless, but constant, she rarely competes with man in the varied departments of science and literature, yet, by her silent labors and gentle teachings, she often rules the fate of empires and decides the destinies of kings.

The evening I left you at your residence, I had no idea that in forty-eight hours I should become so much of an alarmist as to leave New-York so hurriedly. But when people are so congregated and necessarily so many in one room, as at the Institution, the liability to contagion is greatly increased. I believe you purpose remaining in the city during the entire season. May God protect you, and, among his richest blessings, prolong your invaluable life. I am going to a remote part of the country, where the mountains lift their heads and stretch out their arms to protect; and the river that flows at their feet has never borne on its wave the breath of disease: still insidious cholera may come even there.

* * * * * * * * *

Le Roy Female Seminary, July 13th, 1849.

DEAR MARY:—Nearly 2500 years ago the Persian armies, commanded by Xerxes, entered ancient Athens, and in an evil hour behold that great city wrapped in flames; its walls broken, and its white marble edifices and temples, dedicated to the gods, enveloped in smoke and marked for ruin. Where so late art and science, life and beauty reigned, destruction, fire, darkness and decay made their homes. Now the meanest reptiles crawl in the halls of kings, and solitary toads go noiselessly over the banquet floors—and the dark bat sleeps where the birds of Jove plumed their glittering wings—and the moss and ivy grow and feed upon the dust of princes—and the owl, sacred bird of the Athenians, for ever booms above its ruins.

Seven years since Miss Wright, from this seminary, went to Smyrna to teach the Protestant children of the Mediterranean. After a term of four years, she left Smyrna and came to Athens, where she remained two years, and gathered meantime this choice collection of relics. They are placed on shelves in a sort of closet with glass doors; it says over the top, "Athenian Case;" for there are several other similar cases in the room, one of minerals, another of shells, &c. Yesterday Miss Wright took them all down, and placed them one after another in my hands, and described them so perfectly, that it seems to me I have really seen them. And Mary, to-day I will in fancy do the same for you. First, here is a little clay lamp, which was dug from the ruins; you see it is shaped like the half of a goose-egg, and about as large. It has a little tube on the top of one side for the wick, and some little holes in the middle, where the oil was poured in; and they answered also for a vent. It is a rude thing, but we cannot know what great purposes it has answered in the world. Perhaps by its light Aristophanes wove his brilliant comedies. Or it may have belonged to Plato, and sat upon his little classic table, while he wrote his dialogues and twelve letters; the elegance, melody, and sweetness of which, you know, so pleased the people, that they entitled him the Athenian bee. Let us see; Socrates' father was a statuary, and for several years the great philosopher followed the same employment. Here is one of the Athenian gods, and perhaps it was chiselled by his own hand, and one of those which he was afterwards accused of ridiculing; which to us would seem a very slight offence, but then nothing could atone for it but death. In the old world, as in the new, innocence was never safe; since time began she has been exposed to the tongue of slander. Socrates was adorned by every virtue and stained by no vice, and his high-souled independence and freedom of speech upon all subjects, for many years placed him beyond suspicion and malevolence. But after the witty and unprincipled Aristophanes had once ventured to ridicule the venerable character of Socrates in one of his comedies upon the stage, the way was opened, and praise soon gave place to criticism and censure. Envy hurled at him her poisoned arrows, and jealousy, in the voices of Miletus, Aritus and Lycon, stood forth to recriminate him; and good Socrates was summoned before the tribunal of five hundred, accused of corrupting the Athenian youth, and ridiculing the many gods which the Athenians worshipped.

Here, Mary, is a little earthen bowl, which does not seem to differ much from the pottery of our day, though it has lain under ground more than two thousand years. If not the same, it was probably one like it, from which Socrates drank the poison handed him, you remember, by the executioner, with tears in his eyes: then the great moralist exclaimed, there is but one God, and drew off the fatal draught. This, too, is a singular little thing; likewise a piece of pottery shaped like a candlestick, with a bilge in the middle, and a hole in the top. The Greeks called it lachrymatory, which signifies a vessel for tears. What idea those people had of bottling tears, we know not, but it reminds me of the beautiful passage of David, "Thou tellest my wanderings; put Thou my tears into Thy bottle; are they not in Thy book?" These little tear-bottles are found in the sarcophagi, or the stone coffins, dug so frequently from the ruins of ancient Athens; placed there by the friends of the deceased, and probably contained the tears of the mourners, or those whose profession it is in oriental countries to weep for the dead.

Miss Wright was present on one of these occasions, and such control over the lachrymal glands she never before saw: from perfect indifference, they were the next moment seemingly lost in the deepest grief: their cheeks bathed in what *we* call *crocodile tears.*

Here is one of the little sylvan gods of the ancient Greeks, of pottery mould. It was probably a votive offering to Pan and Apollo, suspended perhaps in their caves, which are now to be seen in the side of the Athenian Acropolis, which literally means the highest point of the city. Here is another more ancient still. It must have been used in the days of Cadmus, from its resemblance to the Egyptian mummies. It is a fantastic little thing, marked with hieroglyphics, with arms folded across its breast, and robed like a mummy.

Now open your hands wide, Mary, do not let it drop; *this* is the head of a great lion, taken from the eaves of the Parthenon, the most beautiful temple ever dedicated to the goddess Minerva; and it is still the model of architects all over the world. Put your hand in his mouth, here, you see it is wide open where the water spouted out. It was chiselled from a block of Pentelican marble, which in the quarry they say is pure white and glistens in the sun like rock sugar.

Now I will give you a little marble book. It came from Mars Hill, where Paul stood and declared to the Athenians the unknown God, and defended himself before the Court Areopagus, and answered in the presence of the Athenian judges, for his bold innovation upon their religious faith. Four hundred years before Christ, Socrates was tried and condemned upon the same spot and for the same cause. And a few years since, Dr. King, our missionary in Greece, was tried for a like offence, which, you see, makes him the third in an illustrious line of criminals. When Dr. King went to Athens, he built his house upon a pile of the old ruins, from which he dug this water-jar. It is an ancient thing, but at the present time Greek maidens use them, only larger, for carrying water from the fountains. They have double handles, and when they are filled they hold them in their hands, one on each shoulder, which to us would be a wearisome task; but their supple joints do not mind it, and if we too had some such *exercise*, our forms would perhaps be more erect, and our chests more expansive.

This little stone is a bit of mosaic, taken from the floor of the old temple dedicated to Ceres, at Eleusis, twelve miles from Athens. Anciently this temple was visited by the Athenians annually, in great processions, to pay their adoration to the goddess Ceres; the road to it was called the "sacred way."

Now, Mary, we come to a shelf full of Turkish things, from Smyrna, Asia Minor. Some large dolls, representing the Turks and Armenians in their different costumes; the chibouc or long pipe; and the nigaele, which is a glass vase beautifully painted. When used, it is filled with water; and it has a little fire-place in the top, where the tobacco is burned, and from which the smoke comes down into the water, keeping it constantly bubbling, and then passes off through a long elastic tube, the end of which the smoker has in his mouth, and may sit across the room if he like. This and coffee-sipping, you know, are the Turks' greatest luxuries. By the way, here are some of their cups and saucers, not saucers, but zarfs, little metal stands for the cups, gold or silver, as they can afford. This cup holds about as much as an American would drink at one swallow, but a Turk would be an hour sipping it and blowing it into the smoke of his pipe. Not long since, a traveller from our country called at the house of a Pacha in Smyrna; when helped to this mark of hospitality, instead of holding it gracefully between his thumb and finger, and sipping it gently, he seized it with his whole hand, and drank it off at once, much to the annoyance of the good Pacha, who of course thought his guest greatly wanting in etiquette, and asked his attendants, "Who is this barbarian?" "Let us do what we are going to do quickly, and be off," is every where the characteristic motto of the American.

Dear Mary, you will be weary if I take time to tell you of all these curiosities, and their many associations. But these little Turkish amulets are so very curious. They are made of glass, like small bells, and are worn upon the donkeys and camels, to keep off the "evil eye," as they say, or the influence of jealousy and envy. The children wear them also, for the same purpose. A little daughter of one of our missionaries, who, of course, wore no such badge of oriental superstition, was visited by some of the natives; who, after lavishing upon the fair one their extravagant praises of her beauty, spit in her face, to prevent her being flattered, which was doubtless a very effectual preventive to her vanity.

Matthew says of the Pharisees, "they do all their works to be seen of men, and make broad their phylacteries." Well, here is a phylactery too, and a great many other Roman relics, among which is a box of choice needle-work of gold and silver embroidery, which we could appreciate better if we could see. Beside, Mary, we would like to take a peep into this case of minerals, which extends across the entire room. Like every thing else, this cabinet had its beginning. Twelve years ago a gentleman presented the Preceptress a few stones picked from a quarry in this neighborhood, which have been gradually accumulating, until now this room is a casket of curiosities. About that time, the school was founded by Miss Marietta and Miss Emily Ingham from Massachusetts—and ever since they have been gradually enlarging and improving their building and increasing its advantages, until at present there are few schools in the United States which afford greater facilities for the education of young ladies. Its libraries are large and select, and the conservatory is of itself a little world of beauty and thought. Professor Stanton, who is at the head of the school, is a well-known Artist. His gallery and studio are hung with choice paintings, both by the old Masters, and the work of his own hand. A teacher of painting here, is a lady who has been always deaf. They say when she is kneeling at the easel, her whole soul seems inspired with the beauty of her art, and the forms she leaves upon canvas appear to kindle at the glances of her eye.

Mary, I do sometimes really doubt whether or not, when *properly* considered, it is a misfortune to be blind. Is not our whole nature improved, and our immortal being elevated through this privation? Our sense of feeling becomes so delicate, and such a source of

instruction and new pleasure. Only think of Miss Cynthia, she can feel distinctly the lines and spaces of ordinary printed music. And our hearing is so quickened, and our imagination so fleet, and memory *too*, what new power she possesses, and how tenaciously she clings to every thing, often astonishing even to ourselves. And beside, we know that our feelings are more sensitive, and our attachments stronger and more lasting; and there are few fields of intellectual research in which we may not enter and compete successfully with those who see. * * * *
* * * * *

Rochester, April 11, 1848.

My good friend Mr. D.:—Your long looked for, and thankfully received letter has till now remained unanswered, but not because I have been unmindful of its kindly contents. I was indeed both sorry and surprised to learn that you have resigned your station as one of the managers of the ——, knowing as I do your former devotion to its best interests. But my acquaintance with you, Mr. D——, assures me that you took not such a step, without good reasons for so doing.

The success of benevolence and religion, is not wholly dependent upon the efforts of man. God can work and none can hinder, and in due time the labor of his hands shall be accomplished. But, Mr. D——, when I think of being again barred within those massive walls, my heart sinks at the thought of your coming there no more, to heighten with your presence our pensive joys. Oh! I fondly hope you will visit us sometimes, and let us feel the pressure of your friendly hands, and the cordial greeting of your endearing words. I have passed the winter with my Rochester friends. Spring has come, and it is decided that I take the cars on the first May morning, for the New-York Institution.

A shadow of sadness nestles in my heart when I picture the future; but we see not as God sees. It is a part of my faith that what ever *is*, is for the best, so I manage to put on as sunny a face as possible, and laugh when they speak of my returning, and resuming my labors as a noviciate. We have had a charming winter, and the last twelve days have been exceedingly fine. Lizzy and Carry are busy bossing their gardeners, so I have had an opportunity of passing much of my time out of doors. My general health is very good, but alas for these poor eyes! I much fear they will never recover from the severe blows and coal fires of the Institution.

Glad to hear that Mrs. B. and her family are well. I shall write her soon. Please share my heart's most affectionate regards with Mrs. D. and the other members of your family, and believe me ever gratefully yours.

Long Island Water-Cure, Aug. 31, 1848.

My most excellent friend Mr. D.:—You may think me unmindful of the many demands upon your time. Mrs. N. replied, after reading your last, that she would be most happy to be the bearer of a note to you, an opportunity which I cannot let pass. Dr. N. is certainly one of the choicest spirits I ever knew. He greets me every day with "how do you do, my child?" so affectionately, that I am getting to love him with my whole heart. Mrs. N. is very like him. Fanny Forester and and several other *lights of the age*, were pupils of hers. Mr. D., I am certainly very happy here, and perfectly satisfied with every thing as it is. I wrote you the other day by Mr. E., did you get it? All is going on now as then, only the water is growing colder, and I am every day stronger and can walk farther. With as much grateful affection as my heart can give, I send you this brief note. I cannot tell you how very, very glad I am to hear from you. Your missives, as you call them, are precious things; all here love to read them; indeed we are so out of reading matter, that old letters are sometimes resorted to for pastime. The other day Mrs. N. read me all of yours, often exclaiming as she read on, "What a blessed man that Mr. D. is; I certainly must know him."

Oh, every body is so kind to me! Thank you for that sweet assurance, that *this darkness* does not cloud the hearts of my friends, that it does not make them love me less; their love and sympathy are all that bind me to earth. They are God's gifts, and I do prize them. They spring up every where now, but will it be always so? God grant it may! Heaven bless you, and all yours!

Cousin Will:—I am glad you have at last begun to paste your scraps. I have written, according to your request, the following little address, which if you please you may copy neatly, and place upon the first page; and when your book is completed, I will write for you the close. The accompanying engravings are some which I selected for my own use, but I do not care for them now. You must border them with gilt, and intersperse them through your book; they will both relieve and ornament its pages.

TO MY SCRAP-BOOK.

I found thee amidst a multitude—a nameless, blank, unmeaning thing; with a look expressing nought but cold neglect. Perchance it was pity moved me; or the kind feeling of the good Samaritan. Be that as it may, I passed thee not by, but have brought thee to my own home; and henceforth WE will be FRIENDS, dwelling together in unity and love. Thou shalt be to me a silent companion, sharing all my joys and sorrows; and I will gather for thee from the storehouse of knowledge; I will enrich thee with the unfading beauties of thought—with treasures of intellect; and the holy fires of feeling and love, hope and ambition, too, shall be thine. Upon thy heart will be written indelibly the laws of gratitude and the great rule of right; and thou wilt speak a language pure as lisped by angel-tongues. Thy lessons of wisdom I will make the mottoes of my life. I will bind them about my heart, and be governed by them in all my ways. Thou wilt reason, too, and reflect; and oft, as we onward journey, when Silence holds her spell-like reign, thou wilt turn my free thoughts backward, far o'er the current of years, gathering for me all life's scattered sweets into one hour.

The Poet's art shall be thine; and, more eloquent than lyre of purest note, thou shalt sing of Him who sits in majesty enthroned, whose hand has gemmed the upper skies, and given the rose its tint. For my sadder hours, thou

"Wilt weave a melancholy song;
And sweet the strain shall be, and long—
The melodies of death."

This is a changing world. Those whom we learn to love, die; and thou wilt chronicle for me their departure, and keep in memory their virtues. Earth has many sorrows; and when the dews of feeling gather on my heart, and glisten in my eye, thy treasured words, in kindness spoken, shall be music in my ears; and when years are multiplied, and my hand has forgotten to act, and my heart ceased to feel, thou shalt have a place in my library with the ' world's illustrious," companioned with the mighty minds of old, whose names with thee shall be familiar as household words.

Too often the promises of men, like music, when passed, are obsolete; and we know that "passing away!" is the language of earth; besides, we are not the keepers of ourselves, nor the rulers of our own ways. But what I have promised, that will I do; and after many days, thou shalt bear witness that, like the faithful Samuel of old, "I KEPT MY WORD." * * * * *

P. S. Cousin Will, this is St. Valentine's day. I wish I could write you something that would so strike the chord of cherished memories, as to make your heart vibrate for ever to their pleasant melodies.

My little pet Nickie is recovering; so for a

time heaven will have one angel less, but Mrs. B——'s circle has one more, and may it be long ere it is broken.

New-York Institution for the Blind, June 16, 1849.

The Chief of the Ojibeway tribe, during his recent stay in New-York, gave us a call. His very tread is majesty, and, while being escorted through the house, he stopped to shake hands with every one, and spoke so tenderly to the little boys and girls, that they were moved even to tears. He told those who held their heads down, that if the Indians had them they would lash them to boards to make them grow straight. When all were assembled in the Chapel, Mr. Chamberlain introduced him. Then Miss Cynthia arose, and in her own sweet voice, welcomed him as follows:—

Oh, welcome, thou stranger, our hearts' warm emotions
Are clustering round thee, thou Chief of the brave;
We dream of the hour when with holy devotion,
Thy people first welcomed our sires from the wave.

* * * * * *

We love thy harangues, thy war-song and story
Thy pine-wooded forests, so leafless and drear,
The red child of Nature, that bursts forth in glory,
To chase from its covert the fleet-footed deer.

But mostly, we cherish the heart where the spirit
Hath planted its impress, all deathless and bright,
For the children of promise by birthright inherit
The fountain of knowledge that gloweth with light.

But, *sire*, thou wilt leave us ; when absent, remember
The hearts who have welcomed thy coming to-day,
And fondly will pray for the fate of thy people,
Whose children, like spring-time, are passing away.

To which the great Chief replied so beautifully and so affectingly that I can give you no conception of his words. He speaks English imperfectly, but his figures and illustrations are so fine—nearly every sentence had in it some picture from Nature, gathered by her own child. The master spirits of olden time, the thunders of whose eloquence shook the Grecian forum and awed the world, were from the forest; and like them the chief of the Ojibeways studied beneath the broad canopy of the sky, by the light of the myriad stars, and gathered his imagery amid the cloud-capped hills of the West, where the red man in his native pride follows the buffalo in chase, and where Missouri's waters in *prism* beauties dash, steers his bark canoe.

Speaking of his brethren of the forest, he said: "Nature has given the Indian a great and good heart, and if you would know what religion and learning would do for him, hold a diamond in the sunbeams and watch its sparkling. True, my people see the glories of yonder sun, and dance with delight when he comes up from the waves; but a far brighter light shines in upon your minds. You have learned of God and the Bible, and I hope when the shades of night have fallen on the world, and you go to rest, and the angels are leaning over you listening to your whispered prayers, you will not forget the children of the forest. And when the morning breaks may blessings fall upon them like showers of rain drops upon withered flowers."

A fly might as well try to take the altitude of a mountain, as for me to attempt to give you an idea of his eloquence. His object in passing through the country is to excite, if possible, an interest in behalf of his wronged and oppressed people. At the next session of Congress he purposes petitioning Government for a tract of land in the Northwest Territories, which shall be to the Indian an inheritance for ever, to be neither bought nor sold by any nation. Then, with proper efforts, he thinks civilization, agriculture, the arts and sciences, religion and refinement, may be introduced among them with comparative ease.

In the course of his remarks he exclaimed: "Upon whose grounds do your proud institutions rest? Where dug you the stones of which they are piled, and from whose forests were their timbers hewed? Who welcomed your fathers from the sea, and whose wigwams hid them from the storm, their enemies, and beasts of the wood? Who smoked with them the pipe of peace, and showed them lakes and streams running like silver currents upon the bosom of the earth, and when their French foes came down from the north with battle-axe and spear, who, like the Chief of the Mohawks, harangued his braves, and bared his own breast, and nobly fell in their defence? But oh! we will speak no more of this. Too many of our sires sleep side by side in their angry blood where they fell. The Indian has done evil, but he has sometimes done good; and how much he has been wronged, the Great Spirit and his angels only know. When I look over these grain fields, so far as the eye can reach, my aching heart asks, What has my people received in return? What have the pale faces given in exchange for all these garden scenes? They have taught our lips to thirst for fire-water instead of our mountain springs, and our bows and arrows we have laid down for the white man's thunder-sticks, and no more can we chase the fleet-footed deer, or follow the fox to his hole, or the wolf to his cave; for we are weary and our spirits do fail, and our hearts grow sick and die within us."

The Indian is not all of savage mould; the highly significant names he left upon our lakes and rivers is sufficient index to his perceptions of the beautiful. Who, speaking a language that expresses every shade of thought, could have conceived a more fit appellation for the placid waters of a lake than Winnipiseogee, which means a smile of the Great Spirit? By the light of his own unassisted reason, the Indian has come to know and feel that there is a God, whom he ignorantly but reverently worships; he marks his fierce wrath in the whirlwind, and hears his anger in the thunder's roar; he sees his displeasure in the waning of the moon, and feels his love in the warmer light of the sun.

Institution for the Blind, 1849.

My noble friend Marion:—It is Saturday, teacher's holiday, and Sibyl is, as usual, with her mother. Mr. Stevens, from the Theological Seminary, called this afternoon to favor us with some reading sent us by Dr. Turner, and the last two hours Miss Cynthia and I have listened in raptures to the beautiful poem "Oberon," a translation from the German of Wieland; and when we came to where Huon and Rizia had crossed the fearful mountain, and landed safe in the hermit's vale, I engaged my friend's hand wherewith to write you.

Marion, I have no claims upon either your sympathy or regard. If there is any loveliness in my nature, I am sure my actions never revealed it to you, for dependence has always made me act the part I would not act. In my seeing days, I was proud and resolute, like yourself; no barriers were too high for me to surmount, no difficulties too hard to remove. Once convinced where the path of duty lay, thither my spirit perseveringly trod; but now darkness has made my soul a cellar plant, and its most enduring energies are marked with weakness.

I often pause and wonder for what Providence is preparing me; what order of spirit must I be, that this course of discipline is needful? Whither would my footsteps have led me, if darkness had not set them to wandering? The way I once pursued to happiness is hedged up; but God has mercifully opened another, and though it is a mountain way, and often rough and barren, yet some little fountains of joy do well up along my path, and always too, where I least expect them.

I have recently set my hand to a little work, and, dear Marion, am I presuming too much upon your disinterestedness, when I ask you to aid me? The influence of the good is always desirable, but especially so in an undertaking where success is in the least doubtful. You number in your list many friends, and hoping you will be pleased to gather among them a few subscribers for the volume I am about to publish, I send you the accompanying prospectus. If in your heart it meet with a cordial reception, some names must grace its pages. I am to remain here until my book is published. Many of the good and great are aiding me, and they say I am bound to succeed.

My regards to Mrs. L——, and my love to Lizzie, who first walked with me to church after I could not see, and Mary, who led me first among the flowers, and I called her *Teary*, because she wept with me. And Carrie, who sold her pretty veil to buy for me some shoes; I shall never forget my baker friend, who sent me the gold, nor Franky dear, who returned her watch to the jeweller's, to place some money in my purse.

I love to remember those good souls, Mrs. Sparks and Miss Crane, who watched by me so many long and painful nights. Though I never see them more, and get tidings from them only at long intervals; still, like the Pyramids of Egypt, I know they are there, and unchanged.

There are less true friends in the world for want of a proper knowledge of what constitutes real friendship, than for any defect in purpose. A true friend, is one who would defend *you*, when he would allow himself to be wronged; is incensed at an outrage upon your character or rights, when if it were himself, he would hardly heed it; and while he regrets your errors frankly admonishes you, and then bears with your weaknesses as if they were his own. Some persons make friends with you to-day, but to-morrow with the slightest pretext withdraw their favor. Perchance you have uttered a sentiment, or taken a liberty that does not accord precisely with their views; or some others have expressed opinions derogatory to your worth, and behold they are gone. And yet there is little room to censure them, for love is not always perennial; and when the sun has ceased to shine warmly upon it, nothing is more natural than that it should die, as the leaves wither and fall when the storms of winter pelt upon the trees.

But, dear Marion, when I look into my own heart, and see how imperfectly I have ever filled the offices of a true friend to any one, I feel whatever I may say upon the subject is but a tirade against myself. Indeed nothing short of an elevated nature, and a redeemed heart, can make us perfectly disinterested in any relation.

Modern philosophy and religion teach that the world is rapidly growing better; if so, the time will come when it may be said of all who profess to be friends, like Saul and Jonathan, "In their lives they were lovely and pleasant, and in their death they were not divided."

* * * * * * * *

Raphael never wrote any unwelcome news

to those he loved, nor did he leave an ugly picture on canvas; he said there is a bright and dark side to human life, and when the light has left us, it is better to bring it back by imagination, than mourn over its absence.

* * * * * * *

For a farthing one can buy a song, and there is no good thing in this world that money will not purchase, save a heart that always beats in unison with one's own; and is right out with every thing, faults and all. With such souls, as Mrs. G—— says, we do not converse, but *talk*, lay aside all ceremony, cast off restraint, and word our thoughts as they occur, and our feelings just as they spring, spontaneous from the soul; but such spirits we seldom meet, for like all that is good in this life, they linger by the way, and we have little cause for surprise when they leave us early. In writing, we only hit at things, instead of expressing them freely; this morning I would love to transmit to you a true copy of my troubled feelings, for I know that you would sustain me by your assurances, and I should be profited by your counsels.

Good-by, Marion, that our heavenly Father may bless you, and keep you always in his love, is the prayer of your friend,—

S. H. De K——.

THE END

www.ingramcontent.com/pod-product-compliance
Lightning Source LLC
LaVergne TN
LVHW011218110826
845150LV00006B/1468
9781425516543